Assessing Men Who Sexually Abuse

of related interest

**GOOD PRACTICE IN RISK ASSESSMENT
AND RISK MANAGEMENT 1**
Edited by Hazel Kemshall and Jacki Pritchard
ISBN 1 85302 338 8
Good Practice Series 3

**GOOD PRACTICE IN RISK ASSESSMENT
AND RISK MANAGEMENT 2**
Edited by Hazel Kemshall and Jacki Pritchard
ISBN 1 85302 441 4
Good Practice Series 5

**PSYCHIATRIC ASSESSMENT
PRE AND POST ADMISSION ASSESSMENT**
Valerie Anne Brown
ISBN 1 85302 575 5
Forensic Focus Series 8

**CHILD ABUSE AND CHILD ABUSERS
PROTECTION AND PREVENTION**
Edited by Lorraine Waterhouse
ISBN 1 85302 408 2
Research Highlights in Social Work Series 24

**SEXUAL ABUSE
THE CHILD'S VOICE
POPPIES ON THE RUBBISH HEAP**
Madge Bray
ISBN 1 85302 487 2

STRESS IN SOCIAL WORK
Richard L. Davies
ISBN 1 85302 390 6

Assessing Men Who Sexually Abuse

A Practice Guide

David Briggs, Paddy Doyle, Tess Gooch and Roger Kennington

Jessica Kingsley Publishers
London and Philadelphia

Figures 2.1 and 2.2 reprinted from 'Classifying sexual offenders: the development and correlation of taxonomic models' by R A Knight and R A Prentky in Marshall, Laws and Barbaree (eds) *Handbook of Sexual Assault.* Copyright 1990 Plenum Publishing Corporation, New York.

Figure 2.4 reprinted from *Child Abuse and Neglect*, volume 2 from 'Juvenile sex offenders: development and correction' by Ryan, Lane, Davis and Isaac, pp385–95. Copyright 1987, with kind permission of Elsevier Science Ltd, the Boulevard, Langford Lane, Kidlington OX5 1GB, UK.

Figure 14.1 from Thorton, D. and Fisher, D. 'Risk of reconviction algorithm', *Journal of Mental Health*, volume 2, pp105–117. Copyright 1993 Carfax Publishing Ltd.

The right of David Briggs, Paddy Doyle, Tess Gooch and Roger Kennington to be identified as authors of this work has been asserted by them in accordance with the Copyright, Designs and Patents Act 1988.

First published in the United Kingdom in 1998 by
Jessica Kingsley Publishers Ltd
116 Pentonville Road
London N1 9JB, England
and
325 Chestnut Street
Philadelphia, PA 19106, U S A

www.jkp.com

Second impression 1999

Copyright © 1998 David Briggs, Paddy Doyle, Tess Gooch
and Roger Kennington

Library of Congress Cataloging-in-Publication Data

A CIP catalogue record for this book is available from the Library of Congress

British Library Cataloguing in Publication Data

Assessing sexual offenders

1. Sex offenders - Psychology 2. Personality assessment

I. Briggs, David

364.1'53'019

ISBN 1-85302-435-X

Printed and Bound in Great Britain by
Athenaeum Press, Gateshead, Tyne & Wear

Contents

Acknowledgements

We would like to extend our sincere thanks to each of the following people who acted as critical readers, and provided most valuable comments on the first draft: Chris Davis, Neale Dodds, Jean Jones, Esther Kelsey, Amanda Love, Chris Mackie, Katy Peaden and Alan Peggie.

To Val Milburn for word processing the text and coping valiantly with the many and repeated alterations over time.

To Carol Wake and Jo Summers for some last minute changes to the text.

To several members of the Northumbria Probation Service computer section for their help, and in particular to Sue Bingham and Ian McAdam.

To Sharon Keeble and Adrienne Coleman for their professionalism.

To Liz Rodgers for helping to track down some obscure articles.

To the Northumbria Probation Committee for their encouragement and support.

To Myra, James, and Stuart Briggs for their tolerance.

Introduction

It is no exaggeration to say that there has been something of a revolution in society's understanding of the true nature and extent of sexual abuse over the past fifteen years or so. Ignorance, disbelief, denial, minimisation and collusion have rapidly been replaced by bewilderment, shock, anger, outrage and a demand for vengeance and that something be done to protect the public in general and our children in particular. This has been mirrored by the media portrayal of sexual abusers as 'Beasts' or 'Monsters' and the fact that it has become the normative public response to call for castration, life imprisonment or even the death penalty for those few cases (generally estimated to be less than 10%) which are successfully identified and prosecuted by the Criminal Justice System. Whilst this is readily understandable as a response to society's attempt to come to terms with its new knowledge and the horror of it all, a more measured response is necessary if we are to have any hope of successfully reducing the serious harm inflicted by these acts of abuse or 'unspeakable crimes' as Willis (1993) put it:

> 'It is the cost to children of failing to treat their abusers that must be counted above any other cost when we consider the best way forward for child protection.'

and we would say that this is equally applicable to adult victims of abuse.

The revolution in the general understanding suggested above has fortunately seen a parallel revolution in our knowledge of effective methods of working with sexual abusers. That knowledge remains subject to rapid development from which we must continue to learn, but it also gives us confidence in our ability to make a real difference to the prevalence of future victimisation from sexual abuse. It has become increasingly acknowledged that all agencies concerned in working with sexual abuse, whether that be primarily with victims or abusers, share the common aim of reducing the risk of reoffending in order to protect the public. Crucially we would argue that to be effective this work must begin with assessment, be informed throughout by a process of continuous assessment, and end with assessment. To put it simply, if we don't understand the problem we will never find the solution.

This book is therefore intended to be of practical assistance to professionals from all disciplines involved in the assessment of adult male perpetrators of sexual abuse. Whilst many of the methods and tools might be applicable to female perpetrators, we do not presume expertise in this area. The book is a practice guide drawing on the experience of the authors. It aims to provide an overview of the major considerations necessary for practitioners undertaking assessments. It is designed as a basic level text for those who are at the outset of their careers in work with sexual abusers. Specifically, it does not attempt to address the technologies of penile plethysmography, nor the developing assessment 'systems' of workers such as Richard Beckett or David Thornton in the UK. It is divided into three parts.

PART I

Chapter One outlines our values and the research base which form the foundation of the work. It outlines some of the essential elements of professional support necessary for practitioners undertaking assessment of sexual abusers and comments on the importance of the management function within agencies.

Chapter Two provides a critical summary of some of the theoretical models commonly underpinning assessment work with sexual abusers. These are divided into developmental theories and empirical theories, concentrating in particular upon Finklehor's 'four factor' model (1986) and the 'cycle of offending' (Wolf 1985, Ryan *et al.* 1987) as important tools for assessment work.

PART II

Chapter Three addresses, in a practical way, those general procedures and good practice guidelines underpinning the process of assessing sexual abusers. Beginning with guidance about interviewing, the chapter develops to review the use of questionnaires, penile plenthysmography, projective testing, behavioural observation and other approaches to assessment. The chapter provides an overview of the approach to assessment and forms the basis upon which specific issues are considered in Part III.

Chapter Four deals with some key contexts within which assessments are undertaken. The areas covered are: civil proceedings, child protection conferences, mental health, hostels, pre-sentence reports, prisoner release considerations, and 'Schedule One' offences. Under each of these headings the basic framework within which assessment work may be called for is outlined, with references for these to be pursued in more detail where appropriate. The implications for work in relation to sexual abusers within these contexts are then explored.

PART III

In this final Part, chapters Five to Thirteen examine in turn each of the main areas of the abusers' functioning which might form the substance of the assessment task. Each of these chapters follows a common format examining

why to assess that area, the **targets** for assessment, **how** to assess (with MEASURES where available), and concluding with **tips** and **hints** which the authors have found to be of practical benefit.

Chapter Fourteen examines the vexed question of Risk Assessment but shows that by drawing upon the material within the previous chapters of the book this is a task which we can and should approach with confidence.

PART I

VALUES, RESEARCH
AND THEORETICAL BASES

CHAPTER ONE

Requirements for Effectiveness

Working with sexual abuse is no easy task. The particularly damaging effects of abuse upon its victims places a high burden of responsibility on those practitioners undertaking work with abusers aimed at reducing the risk of further abuse. In addition, the content of the work itself, because of its abusive and sexually explicit nature, can exact a high toll on workers. For these reasons, if we are to aspire to effectiveness in this work we must be clear about why we are doing it, we must ensure that we, and our colleagues, are adequately equipped and supported, and the work must be effectively managed. This chapter will examine each of these requirements in turn under the headings of:

- value and research base
- practitioner support
- management issues.

VALUE AND RESEARCH BASE

At the foundation of our value base is the belief that sexual abuse involves the abuse of power in all cases and the abuse of trust in most cases. Sexually abusive behaviour is not an illness and therefore cannot be 'cured'. It is however behaviour over which abusers can learn to exercise control, and we approach our work with a belief in the capacity for people to change.

Sexual abuse represents distortions in both sexuality and emotionality in the abuser, distortions which are usually best understood in terms of the distorted life experiences and previous learning of those abusers. These factors are important and inform our belief that the perpetrators of abuse must be required to take responsibility for, and constructively address, their offending behaviour, but in so doing deserve to be treated with dignity and respect. We must avoid seeing abusers as nothing other than 'sex offenders' and remember that this is only one aspect of their lives. It is vital that we do this not only because of the moral imperative but also because there are reasons to believe that this approach is more effective in producing the changes in behaviour necessary for the protection of potential future victims (Beckett *et al.* 1994).

We have a shared responsibility to engage the perpetrators of sexual abuse in work aimed at reducing the likelihood of further abuse. The effects of sexual abuse upon its victims are inevitably damaging, usually very traumatic and debilitating, and extend beyond them to their families and to others close to them.

Our aims in working with abusers are consistent with those of colleagues working with victims and we therefore seek to work collaboratively whenever possible. These shared aims provide a powerful motivation for our work but at a time when many agencies are facing ever increasing financial constraints and cut backs we need to be able to support our belief in the value of our work by seeking evidence that intervention is effective and therefore worthwhile.

Our work with sexual abusers remains a relatively new and continually developing area. However, a consensus is developing which recognises that a cognitive behavioural approach is effective in reducing recidivism in child abusers. Marshall (1993) and Pithers (1993) have suggested how cognitive behavioural approaches may be extended to work with rapists.

In his meta-analysis of recent treatment studies, Hall compared the long term recidivism rates of treated and non treated offenders and found that the effect of that treatment reduced recidivism from 27 per cent to 19 per cent. He concluded that:

> 'The results of the present meta-analysis suggest that the effect of treatment with sexual offenders is robust, albeit small...' (Hall 1995)

Given that reconviction rates are fairly low within some groups of offenders (notably intra-familial abusers) (Marshall 1990), this represents a highly significant impact amongst those abusers who tend to have multiple victims. In 1992 the Home Office commissioned a three-stage sex offender treatment evaluation project, the STEP Project (Beckett *et al.* 1994). This was the first major study of the effectiveness of the work of community based programmes in England and Wales looking at six probation programmes and one privately run residential facility. A total of 59 offenders were subject to the research which assessed their deviancy levels before and after interventions using a range of attitudinal and behavioural tests. The results merit consideration in far greater detail than we have space for here but of those men who were undertaking the long term treatment programmes, 64 per cent showed a beneficial treatment effect as did 59 per cent of those who completed the short term programmes. Provision was made for the examination of reconviction rates, two, five, and ten years after offenders completed the programmes. The results of the two year follow up were published in October 1996 (Hedderman and Sugg 1996) and the key points are as follows:

- When compared with a sample of sex offenders put on probation in 1990, those referred to the seven programmes evaluated by the STEP team were less likely to be reconvicted for a sexual offence (5% compared with 9%). This difference still held true when differences in the samples were taken into account.

- Of the eleven STEP offenders who were reconvicted, six committed further sexual offences and five were convicted of a non-sexual, non-violent offence.
- All but one of the sexual reconvictions were for a similar or less serious offence.
- None of the 24 offenders who were assessed as having been significantly treated had been reconvicted within two years. This includes nine who were assessed as being highly deviant before treatment.

These results are amongst those which reinforce our belief that focused, systematic and properly evaluated interventions with perpetrators have the potential to reduce further victimisation. Not all clients will benefit from intervention however and there is a risk that some might be made worse by intervention. We therefore have a professional obligation to ensure that our work in this area is rigorously examined against that which is known to be effective and to avoid professional dogma which can be both dangerous and abusive. We also have a professional obligation to develop expertise in work with client groups who are additionally disadvantaged, for example sexual abusers who have learning disabilities.

This latter point is an example of the duty to deliver our practice in accordance with anti-discriminatory principles. Sexual abuse knows no boundaries in respect of intelligence, socio-economic status, race, ethnicity, religion, or disability. The motivations for child sexual abuse should be seen as independent of gender preference. For these reasons the same care must be given to the need to consider anti-discriminatory principles in the assessment of sexual abusers as in all of our work.

As our primary duty in this work is the protection of the public, we must act upon the results of any assessment work undertaken. This means that the usual requirements of client confidentiality must take second place to the needs of public protection. It also means that we have a duty to put into place whatever public protection measures are indicated by our assessments, examples of which are: not recommending community disposals in Court reports unless we consider it safe to do so, and recommending appropriate conditions in Court Orders and prison licences if it is felt that they would enhance protection of the public.

An effective response to sexual abuse rests upon a multi-agency approach. No single agency, profession, or worker, has the sole responsibility or ability to intervene with an abuser; those working with abusers have much to learn from those working with victims and vice-versa. We therefore have a duty to promote and facilitate close inter agency collaboration and co-operation in our work.

Finally but by no means least in importance is the duty of care in this work, not only in respect of clients but equally in respect of workers. There are particular risks both in terms of efficacy and of personal well being, for workers who are poorly trained, unsupervised and unsupported. This leads us onto the final sections of this introductory chapter – Practitioner Support and Management Issues.

PRACTITIONER SUPPORT

When we deliver training courses on working with sexual abusers one of the first exercises we use is to ask the course attenders to identify what feelings they have when approaching this work. This invariably produces a lengthy list in response to the question 'Working with sex offenders makes me feel...', which usually includes the following:

> Angry, Confused, Scared, Disgusted, Unsure, Deskilled, Inadequate, Challenged, Determined, Worried, Responsible etc.

All areas of our work may have tensions, difficulties, and stresses but there are aspects of working with sexual abuse which can greatly exacerbate these problems. The work requires the examination and discussion of the intimate details not only of sexuality but of a sexuality that is abusive and invariably distressing to contemplate. We need to be aware that some of us will be coming to this work with personal, family or friendship experiences, past and present, about which this work may trigger some very difficult feelings or emotions. We need also to be aware that every one of us, however strong, professional or well protected we may feel, is capable of experiencing distress about this subject, often in the least expected way. We therefore have a duty to care both for ourselves and for our colleagues, not only in order that we do our best to look after our own needs, but also in order that we can be effective in what we are trying to achieve.

One very powerful way in which we can all play a positive part in this is by contributing to a healthy environment within our own agencies. By this we mean an environment within which the common problems associated with this work are clearly acknowledged and where a genuinely supportive atmosphere prevails. Morrison (1990) gave us a structure for understanding this by adopting Summit's Child Sexual Abuse Accommodation Syndrome (1983) into what Morrison called the Professional Accommodation Syndrome.

In his study, Summit described how disbelief, blame and rejection by adults were impediments to recovery for sexually abused children. He described the abused child's typical reactions to abuse in those circumstances as progressing through the stages of secrecy, helplessness, entrapment and accommodation to a point where a delayed or unconvincing disclosure of abuse was subsequently retracted because of the response it had received. Morrison adapted this to show how staff working with sexual abuse may be similarly affected. Readers may wish to refer to Morrison's original work for a fuller consideration of these issues but reference to it may also be found in the later publication *Staff Supervision in Social Care* (Morrison 1993) which we would highly recommend to all concerned with the supervision of staff working with sexual abuse. However, our understanding of the key concepts is as follows:

(1) Secrecy and Helplessness
Staff may be reluctant to express their feelings and emotions about their work with sexual abuse. This will be compounded if their employing agency doesn't facilitate or encourage such disclosure. This can occur where for example the prevailing ethos might be that 'we are all professional people, we have all done our training,

we know what we are doing and we should cope with our work without complaining'. Faced with that general attitude staff will feel that they have no option but to keep their feelings secret and carry on as best they can, and are therefore placed in a position of helplessness.

(2) Entrapment and Accommodation

Just as a child may be unable to see her/his abuser as completely ruthless and self serving so staff must see their profession/colleagues/agency as good/caring, in order to validate their membership of the profession. Therefore the worker may blame her or himself and think they are inadequate and not up to the job. She or he becomes entrapped in a value distortion where disclosure or telling the truth would be seen as unprofessional or weak, and denial of true feelings as being strong and coping. In this way the worker accommodates to the situation.

(3) Delayed or Unconvincing Disclosure

It may be that disclosure later takes place prompted by an external trigger. If, for example, it is caused by inter professional conflict it may be accompanied by anger, non coping behaviour, or absence through sickness and this can lead to an unsympathetic response such as 'he is only saying this because he can't cope,' or 'he should never have become a social worker in the first place'. If on the other hand the accommodation has been through working harder and becoming more professional, disclosure can be disbelieved because colleagues or managers cannot believe that so successful and able a worker could be having such difficulties.

(4) Retraction

If a delayed or unconvincing disclosure has been met by disbelief, scepticism or punishment by the agency, this can result in a retraction as the easier option. The worker may make excuses such as 'I am sorry I was just having an off day,' or 'I am fine really I have just been having a lot of troubles at home and things got on top of me'. So the retraction of the disclosure enables the worker to continue, with the pressure from colleagues and managers removed from them. This can easily seem like the easier option in the short term but of course can only serve to store up further problems for the future. It takes little imagination to see that these problems can, and often do, become serious and debilitating, leading to stress, failure to cope, sickness or resignation from the post.

We can clearly see from this that serious consequences may follow if we allow an unsupportive environment to prevail and we all share a collective responsibility to conduct ourselves in such a way that we contribute to a healthy and supportive working environment.

Each agency involved in work with sexual abuse will have its own provision for staff support. We present here the main provisions within the Northumbria Probation Service by way of example as follows:

(1) We begin with a policy commitment that no member of staff will be required to undertake sex offender work unless they express a willingness to do so.

(2) A range of training courses is provided to equip staff to approach this work with confidence.

(3) Resources have been devoted to the provision of a specialist Sex Offender Team which offers advice and guidance to all staff about any aspect of sex offender work.

(4) There is a policy recognition that co-working offers the best model for sex offender work in most instances both in terms of efficacy and staff support, and this is encouraged and facilitated whenever possible.

(5) Support groups are available for staff engaged in work with sexual abuse.

(6) A consultant is appointed for every groupwork session that takes place, one of his/her key roles being staff support.

(7) Access is provided to an external confidential counselling service when requested.

Whatever facilities exist within our different agencies, we have an individual responsibility to use them appropriately and to encourage our colleagues to do so. We all have a duty to identify for ourselves where our sources of support lie and, as Ryan and Lane remind us, '…sexual abuse has enough casualties, colleagues must take care of themselves and of each other' (Ryan and Lane 1991).

MANAGEMENT ISSUES

Managers of course have a particular responsibility, taking account of those factors discussed in the previous section, to ensure that adequate resources and facilities exist to equip and support staff to carry out their work safely and effectively. Morrison (1994) has suggested that the following 'organisational building blocks' provide a checklist of areas which must be addressed in order to achieve that:

- recognition of the need to work with sex offenders
- mandate and legitimisation for work with sex offenders
- structure for policy and practice development and leadership
- philosophy of intervention
- policy and practice guidance
- training for managers and practitioners
- resources and prioritization of service delivery

- supervision and consultation
- staff care policy and provision
- evaluation of practice

In addition however managers will need to consider their own role in relation to the supervision of practitioners undertaking work with sexual abusers. In our experience some managers may feel deskilled in their supervision of practitioners because of the practitioners' greater knowledge in depth about the detail and content of the work involved. We would suggest that managers need to have an understanding of the nature of the work and the issues involved in order to equip them to address their key supervisory functions of support, accountability, and staff development, but need not however seek to develop knowledge of practice expertise beyond that point.

Managers do have a vital role to play in relation to the selection of staff, the provision of access to relevant and adequate training, to sources of consultation and advice about the specialist aspects of the work, to consultancy, and to appropriate support mechanisms. Attention to those issues should ensure that the first requirement of effective work is met, i.e. that it is delivered by well motivated, well trained, and well supported staff.

Whilst managers need not seek to acquire the in depth knowledge of treatment theory and content necessary for practitioners they do have a role to play in ensuring that the work delivered matches the key principles of effectiveness. In particular, risk classification, criminogenic need, responsibility, treatment modality and programme integrity need to be addressed.

- **Risk classification** – levels of intervention both in terms of treatment content and public protection measures should be matched to assessment of the degree of risk posed by the abuser.

- **Criminogenic need** – work undertaken with abusers should be directed specifically at those factors assessed as being directly relevant to the abusive behaviour of the individuals concerned.

- **Responsivity** – the methods of work selected for use should be those to which the individuals best respond.

- **Treatment modality** – the content of the work should be multi-faceted offering a range of methods based on cognitive behavioural and learning theories and skills orientated material.

- **Programme integrity** – it is essential that programmes of work are delivered as intended and, in particular, mechanisms need to be put in place to ensure that problems of programme drift, reversal and non-compliance are avoided.

Readers are referred to the text edited by James McGuire (1995) *What Works; Reducing Offending, Guidelines from Research and Practice* for further discussion of these crucial issues.

Finally, managers will be concerned to put into place, from the outset, mechanisms to ensure that the work is effectively monitored and evaluated.

These mechanisms should be built into the work at the planning stage, and regarded as integral tools to ensure that the desired outcomes are being reached and to provide the basis for changes to be made where they are not.

CHAPTER TWO

Models Underpinning Assessment

This chapter aims to familiarise practitioners with some of the models which have been developed to explain facets of sexually abusive behaviour. We have chosen to give more emphasis to those which we consider give the most assistance to practitioners in understanding and addressing the phenomenon. For wider ranging reviews of theories and models readers are referred to other texts (e.g. Lanyon 1991, Fisher 1994, Marshall *et al.* 1990). We refer below to developmental models which derive from a range of theoretical perspectives to explain why some men may develop to become abusers. Empirical models are described by Lanyon (1991) as 'data driven rather than theory driven' and offer descriptive accounts of sex abusers and their behaviours based on empirical observations. We believe a third group of models can be identified as those which we think represent useful frameworks for intervening and structuring work with sex offenders.

DEVELOPMENTAL THEORIES

Psychodynamic Models

Over the years theoreticians from a number of backgrounds have attempted to explain why some individuals may develop into abusers. Many of these explanations have proved to be limited in aiding understanding of sexual abuse.

Psychodynamic theories built on the work of Freud (1953) and argued that sexually abusive behaviours relate to unresolved desires, conflicts and tensions from childhood. Lanyon (1991) notes that there does not seem to be much agreement about the detail of psychodynamic models and cites Oedipal conflicts, castration anxiety, repression of Oedipal wishes and regression to less mature behaviour as examples of explanations offered for disturbed sexual behaviour. Such theories suffered from lack of clarity about the links between these conflicts and later behaviours, and treatment programmes based on psychodynamic theories proved ineffective (Furby, Weinrott and Blackshaw 1989).

One 'theory' to have received attention in relatively recent times relates to a concept described as 'courtship disorder'. Lanyon (1991) had noted that relatively little attention has been given to the etiology of less intrusive sexually abusive behaviours such as exhibitionism, voyeurism and frottage. Freund (1990) had argued that these offences as well as 'preferential rape' (i.e. rape committed by men who prefer rape to consenting sex) could be conceptualised as a distortion of what he and a colleague (Freund and Kolarskly 1965) earlier described as a typical behaviour pattern which exists in all human erotic or sexual behaviours. The typical behaviour pattern referred to by Freund is described as four phases (not necessarily in the following order and possibly with differential time spans between each). The phases are:

(1) location and first appraisal of a suitable partner

(2) 'pretactile interaction' (e.g. looking, smiling, posturing, talking)

(3) 'tactile interaction'

(4) 'the effecting of genital union'.

In the anomalous behaviour pattern one of those phases is intensified and distorted, and other phases may be entirely omitted. He proposes that:

(1) Voyeurism may be seen as an exaggeration of the first phase (location of partner).

(2) Exhibitionism may be seen as a distortion of normal pretactile interaction.

(3) Frotteurism maybe seen as a distortion of normal tactile interaction.

(4) The preferential rape pattern may be seen as a distortion of genital union, stripped of all pre-copulatory activity.

The reader is referred to Freund (1990) for fuller discussion of these issues.

Family Systems Theories

Family systems theories became fashionable in addressing intra-familial abuse, regarding it as a result of family dysfunction. Bentovim (1988) describes a 'systems model of the initiating and maintenance of sexually abusive behaviour' in which abusive patterns develop in a circular, interactive manner.

Such patterns serve to avoid conflict in some families and regulate conflict in others. Such theories have rightly been criticised for failing to consider power differentials in relationships (Leonard 1975) and have also been described as 'mother blaming' (Smith 1994). As such, caution is advised in applying family systems theory as a cause of sexual abuse. It is helpful however to understand how an abuser in a family may have skewed family dynamics and boundaries in order to effect and maintain the abuse. It is essential to address how these issues need to be changed to protect individuals and manage the possibility of family reintegration if this becomes an issue.

Dominance and Hostility

Feminist writers (Scully 1990, Herman 1990) have proven helpful in stressing the importance of power in relationships. They point out that the vast majority of sexual abuse is perpetrated by males mainly against females, and contend that it is intrinsic to a system of male dominance. Males benefit by women being subjugated, even if they individually do not abuse. Significant numbers of men acknowledge some form of coercive behaviour to achieve sex with unwilling partners.

In one study for example (Malamuth 1981), 35 per cent of a sample of male college students admitted some likelihood of committing rape if guaranteed immunity from detection. On a scale of 1 (not likely at all) to 5 (very likely), 35 per cent rated 2 or above, 20 per cent rated 3 or above. Similar findings were made by Koss and Leonard (1984) and Tieger (1981). Feminist theorists contend that psychological explanations of rape are of little use in understanding the phenomenon. Sexual abuse is at the extreme end of a continuum of male dominating behaviour.

From a different perspective Malamuth, Heavey and Linz (1993) argued that there are significant differences in men who would and would not rape. Their research indicated that predictors of sexual aggression relate to an interaction between characteristics related to promiscuity, and characteristics related to hostility. Characteristics of the 'sexual promiscuity path' include a greater likelihood of the aggressor coming from a home where there was sexual abuse, lack of intimacy, or violence; of the aggressor having sexual intercourse at an early age and of having a large number of sexual partners. Characteristics of the 'hostile masculinity path' include: the abuser needing to control others, hostility to women, a sense of being rejected, a sense of betrayal, difficulty in trusting others, and violent attitudes to women. The model continues to undergo further research and refinement (Malamuth et al. 1996).

Feminist theories focus on the issue of the abuse of power as central in all sex offending, and consequently form a useful context for learning-based theories, in other words by pointing out that much of what individuals learn is from society in general or role models close to us. In this case men who commit sexual offences learn from society's domination of women sexually, and by the role of males, notably fathers, in their lives. It reminds us that the eradication of sexual abuse will require broader interventions, for example in the ways boys are socialised. Much of the argument about power, and men's desire to humiliate as a primary motivator in sexual abuse applies to men who have raped women. McMullen (1990) strongly argues that these factors are also inherent where men rape adult men, and uses a study by Groth and Burgess (1980) to support the position.

Whilst abuse of power is clearly inherent in all forms of abuse, its role as a primary motivator in child sexual abuse is less well argued. Early theories dealt uneasily with findings that there are female abusers, albeit in the minority. Nevertheless feminist theories form an essential strand of the value system of those working with abusers, and remind practitioners of the necessity to keep issues relating to the abuse of power as a focus of the work.

Learning Theories

Theories which have come to prominence in recent years stress the importance of learning in the development of sexually abusive behaviours and related thought processes.

Wolf's (1985) study indicated that offenders have generally had early experience of abuse (i.e. as victims) or at least some form of exposure to abusive attitudes. He argued that these experiences endow them with the potential to become abusive. Those who become sexual offenders in later life are those whose experiences have led them to have low self esteem and who tend to compare themselves with idealised others. They ruminate and retreat into a fantasy life of sexual preoccupation. Distorted thinking generated in fantasy is reinforced through masturbation and sexualised behaviour. Wolf further developed a model conceptualised as a self reinforcing cycle which tends to be well established by the time a repeat adult offender is assessed. Wolf's and other models describing cycles of offending are presented later in this chapter.

Another popular theory integrating the role of learning with biological, sociocultural and situational factors was developed by Marshall and Barbaree (1990). They argue that males have a biologically endowed propensity for self interest associated with a tendency to fuse sex and aggression. The developmental task is to acquire inhibitory controls over this propensity. They argue that the biological influence is reduced by learning but reaches a period of heavy influence during puberty when hormonal changes are dramatic. Levels of hormonal activity may make learning more or less effective.

Within this model childhood experiences are important, particularly where these have included violent and inconsistent parenting. Anti-social sexual fantasies may begin as a result of maltreatment. Sociocultural influences on learning may include general cultural features such as male dominance in society (although Japan, for instance has a male dominant culture but little sexual violence) as well as the availability of pornography.

Marshall and Barbaree argue that most offenders can control their behaviour until situations arise in which they are unlikely to be caught. However they also note that some 'transitory situational factors' are created by the offender himself. These include alcohol consumption, anger levels, prior arousal levels, societal situations including warfare and the manipulation of situations to minimise the risk of being caught.

EMPIRICAL THEORIES

These emerge from attempts to outline the characteristics of sex offenders from researching their behaviours. 'Typologies' of offenders have been developed which serve as an example of this approach.

Sex Offender Typologies

Knight and Prentky (1990) have proposed what is now regarded as the most comprehensive typology of sexual abusers. In organising offenders into different types on the basis of their characteristics they also believe that it will be possible to identify different developmental pathways for different abusers. They have proposed typologies for both child molesters and rapists.

Knight and Prentky's (1990) typology of 'child molesters' theoretically yields 24 different 'types' of child molester, although their early studies indicated that 11 of these types rarely, if ever, occur. Two independent reference points or axes were defined and characteristics identified from each. On Axis I the abuser is characterised as having a high or low level of fixation on children. The second decision is to subdivide each category to identify whether the offender has a high or low degree of social competence as defined by the level of '...success in employment and adult relationships and social responsibilities'.

Axis II is used first to identify whether abuse is characterised by high or low amounts of contact with children. The 'High Contact' group is subdivided to assess whether the abuser's motivation is 'interpersonal' (where the abuser attempts to establish relationships and does not aim to achieve orgasm during the offence) or 'narcissistic' (where the abuser makes no attempt to develop a relationship and the aim of the abuse is to achieve orgasm).

'Low contact' offenders are further subdivided according to low or high physical injury sub types by assessing whether or not physical injury was inflicted upon the victim. The low and high physical injury sub categories are further divided into sadistic (overt or muted) or non sadistic groupings.

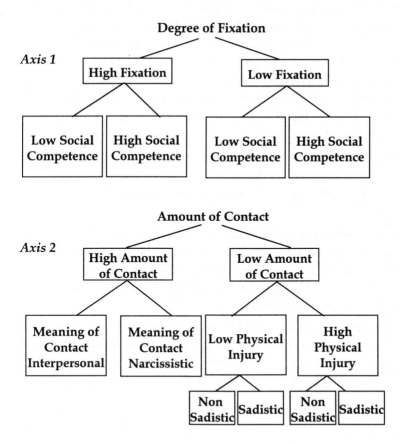

Source: Knight and Prenky (1990)

Figure 2.1 Flow diagram of the process for classifying child molestors

Knight and Prentky (1990) have evolved a similar complex typology for rapists. This appears more comprehensive than those typologies developed earlier, for instance that developed by Groth (1979) who described rapists as motivated primarily by anger, power or sadism. Knight and Prentky identify five types categorised as Opportunistic, Pervasively Angry, Sexual Sadistic, Sexual Non-Sadistic and Vindictive which with the exception of the Pervasively Angry group can be subdivided into Low and High Social Competence groups (although with sadists Low Social Competence correlates with overt sadism, and High Social Competence with muted sadism).

- **Opportunistic** rapes are impulsive, unplanned and predatory, motivated by situational concerns rather than deviant sexual arousal. Impulse control is generalised to all aspects of lifestyle. Gratuitous force or aggression is usually absent. The desire for immediate gratification and disregard for the victim's needs are common features.

- **Pervasively angry** rapists are motivated by undifferentiated anger to women or men. Aggression is gratuitous and may be extreme. Sexual assault is only part of a pattern of generalised aggression, and deviant sexual fantasies are not a general feature.

- **Sexually motivated** offenders whether non-sadistic or sadistic do, by contrast, have sexual and/or sadistic fantasies or preoccupations which motivate the offending, albeit that sex may be fused with aggression, dominance, co-ercion or feelings of inadequacy.

- **Overt sadists** behave similarly to pervasively angry rapists except that more planning is evident.

- **Muted sadistic** types will mainly express sadism symbolically or in fantasy.

- **Non sadistic** sexually motivated rapists are said to exhibit the least sexual aggression (and tend to be less aggressive in non sexual interactions). They may flee in the face of resistance. Fantasies are described as including feelings of inadequacy and distorted 'male' cognitions about women and sex.

- **Vindictive** rapists appear to focus their anger exclusively on women. Behaviours are degrading and humiliating to their victims. They show a lower level of impulsivity than opportunistic or angry types and aggression is not eroticized.

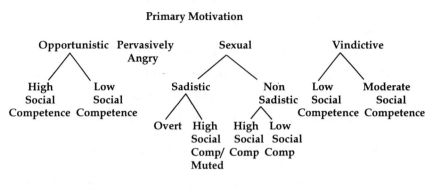

Source: Knight and Prentky (1990)

Figure 2.2 Typology of rapists

Finkelhor Four Factor Model

Finkelhor (1986) and his colleagues collated their research and that of others. Rather than identify typologies they evolved a 'four factor' model of sexual abuse and argued that these factors must exist before sexual abuse can take place. The four factors identified by Finkelhor are as follows:

- A child abuser would tend to find relationships with children in some way emotionally gratifying and congruent (in the sense of the child fitting the adult's emotional needs).

- A child abuser would be capable of being sexually aroused to a child. Indeed some abusers, notably extra-familial abusers, tend to have strong sexual arousal patterns towards children.

- A child abuser would tend to be blocked in relationships with appropriate adults. Clearly this factor alone would not explain sexual abuse without the existence of attraction to children, but it is argued that abusers will have such difficulties. These may relate for example to difficulties in forming peer group relationships in adolescence and feeling more comfortable with younger children, or learning difficulties which inhibit adult relationships.

- A child abuser is not deterred by conventional social restraints and inhibitions against having sexual relationships with a child.

Finkelhor's research related to child sexual abuse, but it is conceptually possible and practically useful to adapt the model to rapists.

Finkelhor subsequently developed a model identifying four 'pre conditions' which must exist before sexual offences are committed. This has been used as a framework for practice which practitioners have found to be invaluable and the four preconditions have been conceptualised as a 'pathway' to abuse. Certainly it is one of the most influential models used by practitioners in Britain to frame assessment of sexual offenders. The four preconditions are identified as follows:

(1) The abuser must have a **motivation** to sexually offend.

(2) The abuser must overcome **internal inhibitions** to offending.

(3) The abuser must overcome **external inhibitors** to offending.

(4) The abuser must overcome the child's (victim's) **resistance**.

First, **motivation to sexually abuse**. Motivating factors identified in the model are:

- The development of emotional congruence with children (i.e. many abusers feel comfortable in the company of children and delude themselves into believing that their relationships with children are based on equality of power and maturity).

- Arousal to inappropriate stimuli such as images of children generally or of specific gender, age or physical characteristics.

- Blocked alternatives. i.e. the inability to form appropriate relationships. (In the case of rapists this may also refer to issues such as anger and mood controls which are dealt with via aggression.)

Second, **overcoming internal inhibitors**. Finkelhor identified a number of ways in which abusers persuade themselves that their behaviour is acceptable and factors which seem to be associated with disinhibition. These include the following:

- **Stress.** This might include financial difficulties, unemployment or bereavement. As with most urges, the urge to offend may be most difficult to control at times of pressure.

- **Rationalising cognitions** (otherwise known as cognitive distortions, distorted thinking or justifications) are the most common way in which abusers justify their behaviour and give themselves permission to abuse. The range of distortions and their role in offending are outlined more fully in chapter seven.

- **Alcohol, drugs and solvents** may be used to disinhibit behaviour and may also be referred to as a justification e.g. 'I would not have done it if I had not been drunk'. Alcohol can also be used to groom and disinhibit victims.

- **Severe personality disturbance or organic factors** (e.g. dementia or head injury). These cases are comparatively rare, but it is possible that brain damage or dementing illnesses can cause poor impulse control.

The third precondition is that of **the abuser overcoming external inhibitors**. Clearly, to secure access to victims and ensure secrecy about their behaviour, abusers must manipulate or 'groom' those around them. Finkelhor identified a number of ways in which this may happen although the list is by no means exhaustive. These examples tend to relate to intra familial abuse. Chapter Five describes some strategies adopted by extra-familial abusers and several studies have addressed this issue (Conte, Wolf and Smith 1989, Dunkerley *et al.* 1994).

- **Geographical and social isolation.** Abusers are often men who are very domineering (particularly within families) and sometimes isolate children and other family members. They prevent children having contact with friends or engaging in social activity. They may also restrict partners' contacts with family and friends.

- **Unusual sleeping arrangements.** Abusers often have the capability to persuade their family or others to adopt the most odd arrangements in order to facilitate abuse. Practical examples are numerous and include from our own practice, a family who were persuaded to let a virtual stranger sleep with their son; a grandfather who shared the spare room with his granddaughter so his wife 'could get a good night's sleep'; and an uncle who shared the spare room with his niece so his wife would not be disturbed as she had to get up early for work.

- **Carers absent.** Abusers frequently exploit the absence of a carer from home, e.g. if a partner works. They may go further and persuade the partner to be absent for apparently sensible reasons which cast the abuser in a good light, e.g. persuading a partner to take her mother out. This 'distancing' is not only physical. Often abusers will skew the dynamics of a family to create rifts and disturb boundaries, so that individuals feel excluded.

- **Sex-punitive parental attitudes.** Despite abusers indulging in sexually highly inappropriate behaviour, they may impose a regime on a family which is highly puritanical. Thus no discussion of sexual matters is allowed and children have no vocabulary with which to raise the issue of abuse.

The fourth precondition relates to **overcoming victim resistance**. Once the first three preconditions are met the abuser must overcome the resistance of the victim. Tactics may range from the most subtle to the most aggressive, often with a complex combination of each. Finkelhor identified the following:

- **The victim's lack of sexual knowledge.** Consequently it is relatively easy to persuade a child that what an abuser is doing is some sort of 'special game'. The child may not even realise that what is happening has a sexual connotation for the abuser.

- **Force.** Abusers sometimes use force in their abuse of children (e.g. by digital penetration, rape etc.) but often use the threat of force to the child or a relative to terrify children into silence. These are often in the nature of 'if you tell anyone your mother will die'.

- **Lack of assertion.** The majority of sexual offences are committed by someone who has taken time building up some sort of trusting relationship with them. Given the inherent power in the relationship it is unlikely that a child will be sufficiently assertive to resist the demands of any predatory adult.

Finkelhor's four preconditions model has been adopted as a framework for both assessment and intervention with abusers. Assessment of the various factors involved is outlined in Part III of this volume and its use in risk assessment is addressed in Chapter Fourteen.

THE CYCLE OF OFFENDING

Another highly influential model for British and North American practitioners has been that of the Cycle of Offending. This addresses similar areas to those identified in the Finkelhor Model but views them as a self reinforcing, or addictive, cycle of thoughts and behaviours rather than a pathway to abuse. The origins of the Cycle framework are not entirely clear and many adaptations are to be found. The literature suggests that Steven Wolf (1988) and Sandy Lane and colleagues (in Ryan, Lane and Isaacs 1987) evolved the concepts separately.

Steven Wolf's model complemented his developmental model identified earlier in this chapter. An abuser's negative self image may be exacerbated by a life event, triggering his retreat into an abusive fantasy life reinforced by masturbation in order to give pleasure and comfort. After rehearsal of events in fantasy gradual moves are made to target a victim and to plan a situation to make it possible to offend. This includes manipulating the environment and overcoming the resistance of the victim. Abuse occurs and with it come strong reinforcing feelings followed by a period of guilt. Distorted thinking reduces the guilt so an abuser reverts to his equilibrium state of low self esteem before another 'trigger' event initiates the move into the cycle again.

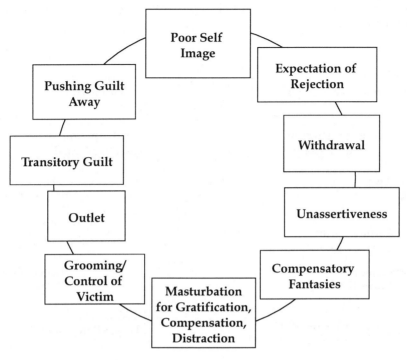

Source: Wolf (1985)

Figure 2.3 The cycle of offending

Lane and colleagues (Ryan *et al.* 1987) also identified developmental factors relating to negative feelings (e.g. unresolved anger or powerlessness) in early years, often related to abusive experiences, and argued that abusive adolescents may compensate for these feelings by victimising others and perceiving themselves as powerful. They argue as follows:

> 'Because of the reinforcing nature of sexual behaviours, the deviant acts of a sexual offender may become repetitive, ingraining deviant patterns which become habitual and may progress to incorporate more and more deviant sexual acts. Reinforcement comes from the thrill of secrecy; the anticipation in fantasizing, planning and stalking; the addictive qualities of seeking more and better 'highs'; and thinking errors which rationalize and support the behaviours. Behavioral reinforcement occurs with the arousal and ejaculation from masturbatory fantasies as well as during the sexual assaults. The perceived positive feelings of power and control combine with physical gratification to out-weigh the potential negative consequences of the behaviour.' (p.387)

The sexual assault cycle developed by Lane is developed from a cognitive/behavioural dysfunction cycle applicable to many maladaptive behaviours. Ryan *et al.* note that the cycle has been adapted by many clinicians with variations. Fisher (1994) notes that whilst Lane's work was specifically developed through work with adolescents it has been widely adopted to examine work with adults.

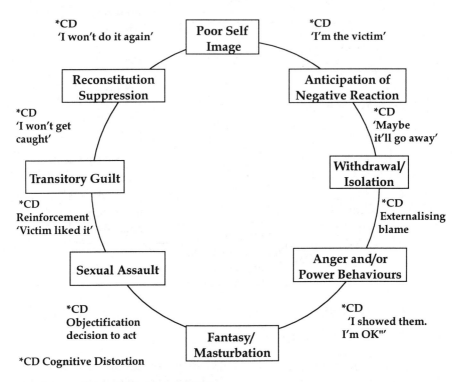

Source: Lane (in Ryan *et al* (1987))

Figure 2.4 The sexual assault cycle

The model, as used in practice assumes that by the time a worker meets a repeat abuser, a self reinforcing assault cycle will probably have been well established over the period of the abuse. The cycle will be inhibited for longer or shorter periods dependent upon a 'trigger' which leads the abuser back into his cycle. In reality the trigger may well be a series of events of significance to the abuser, particularly associated with mood state. These mood states have generally been thought to be negative, but Pithers (1993) indicates that intense positive mood states may destabilise abusers.

Both the Wolf and Lane models are intricate. This has led to considerable adaptation of their models for practical use in assessment. The adapted cycle used by the current authors includes the key stages of the Wolf and Lane models. It has features common to the addictive cycle which most workers and abusers can identify as relating to other addictive behaviours (e.g. smoking, drinking, and habitual overeating), and as such aids understanding.

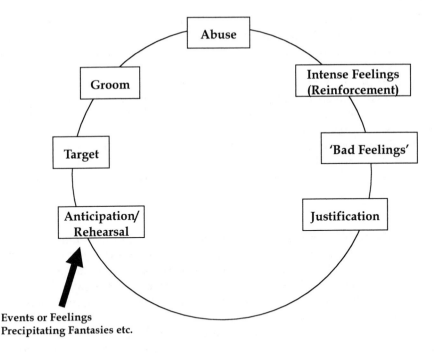

Figure 2.5 Sexual assault cycle

The Stages of the Cycle

ABUSE

The types and numbers of abusive incidents committed by the abuser will vary. An escalating (or less frequently de-escalating) pattern may exist, or abusers may repeat almost identical acts with regularity. The frequency of abuse is important as it is an illustration of the compulsivity of the behaviour. Where abusers have inhibited their behaviour for months or even years they may have good control strategies on which to build. Conversely where an abuser has offended daily (or more) then the necessity for urgent control measures is apparent.

INTENSE REINFORCING FEELINGS

As with all addictive behaviour intense pleasurable feelings relating to the behaviour outweigh concern for longer term, broader consequences, and reinforce the behaviour. Where sexual intercourse to ejaculation occurs, or masturbation during or after abusive acts is evident, then sexual gratification is an obvious emotional outlet. However, a range of feelings is usually apparent combining some or all of the following: emotional closeness, power, a feeling of being in control, excitement, release of anger, revenge (specific or general) or, in the case of sadistic abusers, the enjoyment of inflicting pain.

'BAD FEELINGS'

Theoretical models tend to describe this phase as 'transitory guilt' or 'remorse.' We have adopted the more down to earth terminology as other descriptions tend to imply awareness of harm to victims and a wider impact on others.

Unfortunately, whilst these factors are apparent in some abusers, they are by no means universal. The most common concerns abusers have are fears of the consequences for themselves, notably the fear of disclosure, imprisonment, loss of job, loss of family, and aggression from others.

Feelings of being 'dirty' are common as is a sense of stigmatisation because (unless they are part of a network of abusers) they need to live a lie whilst they are abusing – i.e. condemning abuse in public, whilst themselves abusing in private.

JUSTIFICATIONS

This is the term we prefer to avoid jargon inherent in the academic model where 'cognitive distortions' are described. Most abusers can understand that they 'justify their behaviour' and 'make it seem okay to themselves'. More intellectually limited clients can grasp the concept of 'making excuses' for themselves although the word 'excuses' can be somewhat glib to describe some of the thought processes involved.

The assessment of distorted thinking is described more fully elsewhere (Chapter Seven) so only a brief summary is given here. Justifications adopted can be on a wide spectrum. At one end are fairly flimsy 'excuses' which can be readily debunked. These tend to be those related to the blaming of factors such as drink, stress and lack of sex with a legitimate partner. Justifications at the other extreme may not even be overt, or may be part of a core aspect of an abuser's personality (e.g. a belief that when they themselves were abused, it did no harm, so their abuse of others is not harmful).

ANTICIPATION AND REHEARSAL

Virtually all abusers think about their behaviour before they do it. Even impulsive rapists will have some forethought, albeit maybe fleeting. Structuring discussions in the context of this exercise can 'normalise' the discussion of arousal patterns in groups and individual work. This is also the pivotal point of the cycle where fantasy may move into reality. By fantasising and rehearsing abusive behaviour in his mind an abuser can make his actions seem more acceptable. Except in the case of sadists, fantasies will usually involve victims who are sexualised and enjoying the behaviour.

TARGETING

This flows smoothly from the previous phase as abusers select vulnerable people to abuse. It is important to know which individuals an abuser may choose to target.

The choice of target may be incidental, for instance in many cases of opportunistic or vindictive rapists. Alternatively it may be highly fetishistic. For example, an abuser may have developed a particular specific attraction to pre-pubescent girls in school uniform. The fetish may be specific to boys or girls or may cross gender. In addition, the choice of target may be situational, for instance in the case of a stepfather who develops a fantasy that when she is old enough he will marry and run off with his stepdaughter. Other intra-familial abusers may also target children outside the family, or 'look but not touch'. Conversely some paedophiles are known to target vulnerable families to secure access to children and others target organisations for similar reasons. Whatever the physical characteristics of the preferred target, availability is obviously an issue, and abusers may move from their 'ideal type' if they are not available. Studies by Conte *et al.* (1989) and Dunkerley *et al.* (1994) found that an overriding characteristic of victims was that they were perceived by the abuser as vulnerable (lonely, more tactile, less likely to tell, attention seeking) in relation to other potential targets.

GROOMING

Grooming is the term which has developed whereby abusers gradually 'test out' the level of resistance a victim is likely to pose and secures privacy and secrecy for his actions. The phase can be extremely long, and be part of the build up of excitement or very short immediately preceding the attack, as with some rapists. In the latter case a term such as 'stalking' may be a better description.

There are as many grooming strategies as there are abusers. Some of the desensitisation of victims could even itself constitute subtle abuse. This might include watching pornography with a victim or inappropriate touching or kissing.

The choice of the perceived vulnerable child may be a grooming tactic in itself. Visiting parks during school time will identify children who should be at school so may have personal problems, be subject to little oversight at home and will have difficulty telling (because they should be at school). By selecting a child in a family who may already exhibit difficult behaviour, an abuser can exploit difficult family dynamics and trap a child who might succumb to the attention the abuser may give her or him.

There are an infinite variety of ways an abuser secures physical separation. However there are also more subtle psychological dimensions of the groom-ing process. In families, for instance, an abuser who initially justifies his behaviour by arguing that he and his wife 'do not get on', may in reality have been provoking arguments to keep her at a distance. By inconsistent parenting he may also generate arguments between the victim and her/his mother and/or siblings. Men who abuse in organisations are often well regarded and make themselves indispensable.

The use of this model in practice, the targets for assessment and how to assess are described in Chapter Five.

A MODEL OF CHANGE

So far in this chapter models presented have been those involved in under-standing the development and characteristics of sexually abusive behaviour, and key factors in assessing men who abuse. It is also important to assess at what stage an abuser is in terms of motivation. The work of Prochaska and Di Clemente (1982) has been a pivotal influence in identifying different stages of change. In their work with smokers they identified a series of stages through which addicts pass on their way to controlling behaviour. George and Marlatt (1989) argued that their model could be used to assess stages of change in other addictive behaviours including sexual abuse. The stages are identified as follows:

- **Precontemplation.** During this phase no problem is acknowledged so the relevance of treatment is not considered. During this phase motivational strategies are required.

- **Contemplation.** Where the client begins to consider that there may be a problem. Motivational work continues and some action initiated.

- **Action**. During this phase work is undertaken to change some of the problems which contribute to the addictive behaviours.

- **Maintenance.** The phase in which it is necessary to reinforce the changes made and prevent a reversion to previous behaviour, and manage lapses.

- **Relapse**. Describes times when the client reverts to all or some of the previous behaviours. In sex offender work it is important to address behaviours which may herald a relapse, rather than wait until reoffending occurs. In the relapse phase a client may refer to 'precontemplation' or be determined to continue the work and move back to the contemplation/action phase.

It is intended that the models outlined in this chapter will give the reader an understanding of a range of theories to assist in understanding the development and characteristics of sexual abusers and their abusive behaviours.

Frameworks for assessing the various factors relating to abusive behaviours are also offered, as is a model of change. The practical application of these models as aids to assessment is described in Part III and Chapter Fourteen outlines their use in risk assessment.

PART II

HOW TO ASSESS
Contexts for Assessment

CHAPTER THREE

How to Assess

Part III of this book deals with the practicalities of assessment of particular aspects of the sexual abuser's functioning, that is, functions considered relevant to the longer term management and treatment of clients, as well as functions thought to be relevant to the evaluation of risk. The purpose of this chapter is to outline some of the basic procedures for assessing sexual abusers and to introduce rudimentary guidelines for best practice. Whilst we attempt in this book to present information in as simple and straightforward way as possible, we would caution the reader against adopting simplistic, 'cookbook' approaches to assessment. Assessment is a skill, and if it is to develop like any other it will require practice based on clear feedback from skilled practitioners. Furthermore the skill should be grounded on a sound knowledge base, and the practitioner's preparedness to seek continual improvement.

CONFIDENTIALITY

It is important to be clear with clients about the limits of confidentiality in work with them, before any work is undertaken which focuses on the abusive behaviour. Public protection (particularly child protection) concerns will override concerns for client confidentiality. If workers become aware of offences which have not been processed by the police they will be under a duty to pass on those concerns. This particularly relates to recent offences and past offences where there is an identifiable victim. A decision not to pass on information (e.g. where there is general reference to old behaviours with no identifiable victims) should never be taken by individual practitioners. Reference should be made to agency policy and any inter-agency protocols which exist. If in doubt the case should be discussed with the appropriate department of the Police.

Even where cases have been processed in the Criminal Justice System there may be instances where it is necessary to pass on information. For example, if a man is acquitted of a charge of incest against a daughter but pleads guilty to indecent assault, the case cannot be reopened (except in rare circumstances which are unlikely to apply) on the same facts. However, if the man subsequently admits that he did commit incest it would be helpful to tell those who are working with the victim as it may be helpful in therapy.

Some other behaviours which are not in themselves offences will need to be reported. These will include breaches of probation, parole or restrictions imposed in civil proceedings.

In addition, if a child is perceived as being at risk then the Social Services Department should be informed. It is usually possible to maintain confidentiality in relation to an abuser's own personal details but even this cannot be guaranteed. Situations have arisen for instance where clients have disclosed that they had been abused, and it has become apparent that their abusers still have access to children either through family or work contacts. In these instances it has been necessary to breach client confidentiality.

We stress that the above is only offered as advice and that workers should always work within their own agency policies and any inter-agency agreements which exist.

ASSESSMENT STRATEGIES

It is important to consider the widest possible range of sources of information and opinions in order to develop the most comprehensive assessment and to check one source against another. A range of possible strategies is illustrated in Figure 3.1.

Figure 3.1 Assessment strategies

THE INTERVIEW

The interview is perhaps one of the most useful tools we have to assess sexual offenders, yet paradoxically it is a tool which is often neglected by workers. A skill in interviewing is often assumed following basic training in the professions. It is relatively rare for a practitioner's interviewing skills to be subject to external scrutiny, further training, or refinement, post qualification.

Those skills required in interviewing sexual offenders are highly sophisticated. The purpose of an interview is to determine information of the most reliable and valid sort about the client and aspects of the client's sexuality (in its broadest sense) which will inform us as to risk and options for intervention and management.

There is a clear dilemma for the client however. For the client to disclose reliable and valid information, this means disclosure of embarrassing, potentially damaging and sometimes frightening material. In our work we advise that a careful balance is drawn between support and challenge. Figure 3.2 suggests that various combinations of support and challenge will engender different responses in the client, which in turn will facilitate or discourage disclosure of valid information.

For example, if the therapeutic and working environment created by the worker offers the client considerable support but little challenge, we might expect complacency to arise in the client and for that client to generate some,

High Support

Client Behaviour:	*Client Behaviour:*
Complacent	**Active, Involved**
Comfortable	**Purposeful**

Low Challenge	**High Challenge**
Client Behaviour:	*Client Behaviour:*
Disengaged	**Stressed**
Apathetic	**Superficially Compliant**
Inconsequential	

Low Support

Figure 3.2 Potential client behaviours during assessment as a function of worker support and challenge

though not optimal, information and disclosure. Conversely if the client is given a high degree of challenge with little support (a situation we would term confrontation) this is likely to produce stress in the client, defensive behaviour, and a situation in which the client is likely to 'talk the talk' rather than 'walk the walk' (i.e. slip into providing the worker with information the client feels the worker wants to hear, rather than providing information which is genuine). Worse still is the situation where the worker creates a situation in which both little challenge and little support is offered to the client. In these situations the assessment process is likely to be disjointed, and characterised by apathy and a lack of engagement on both sides.

We strive to achieve a situation where the assessor creates a situation which the client finds supportive, yet one in which the client receives significant challenge along the way.

The following are indicators of the sort of behaviours that might represent both support and challenge within this model.

Supportive Interviewer Behaviour

- praising the client when praise is due
- asking the client how he feels
- acknowledging the client's feelings
- helping the client express his feelings
- expressing positive emotions to the client (warmth, confidence, determination, respect etc.)
- clear contracting of the interview process and scope
- acknowledging the client's strengths.

Challenging Interviewer Behaviours

- being honest with the client about information that is disbelieved
- sticking with difficult subjects even though this might be embarrassing or uncomfortable for the client
- being honest with the client about how his abusive behaviour made the worker feel
- pointing out discrepancies in the content of material presented by the client
- urging the client to go beyond his accepted and 'safe' understanding of his abusive behaviour
- pointing out to the client barriers that he might put in the way of progress and work.

The focus of information gathering during the interview will obviously depend on the purpose of that interview and the model used to underpin the evaluation.

A useful overview of informational targets which might be used when assessing child sexual abuse 'offenders' has been drafted by Faller (1993) on behalf of the US National Centre on Child Abuse and Neglect. The informational targets and rationale for their determination are reproduced in Figure 3.3 below.

	Information	Rationale
(1)	Past history of physical abuse,neglect, etc.	Potential for deficits in nurturing skills, potential lack of empathy with victim
(2)	Past history of sexual abuse	Propensity to become a sexual abuser
(3)	Current living situation	Safety of the alleged victim, other potential victims
(4)	Education and employment history	Index of overall function, including impulse control problems (frequent job changes) and access to potential victims
(5)	Parenting	Ability to provide adequate care (sexual abuse aside), appropriate vs inappropriate investment in the children, distortions in views of children
(6)	Discipline	Possible physically or emotionally abusive behaviour, impulsive reactions, unrealistic expectations of children, blaming alleged victim for allegation
(7)	Partner relationship	Possible abusive relationships and/or serious problems in past or current object relations, potential factors that might increase risk for sexual abuse
(8)	Sexual history	Possible evidence of other paraphilias, availability and use of sexual outlets, level of sexual experience, knowledge and beliefs about sex
(9)	Substance abuse	Substance as a disinhibitor to sexual activity with children, possible use of substance to cope with guilt regarding sexual abuse, link between substance abuse and criminal activity, index of superego and overall functioning

(10)	Mental illness	Potential for delusional system justifying sexual activity with children, index of overall functioning
(11)	Mental retardation	Potential source of problems in judgement or impulse control, index of overall functioning, blockage of gratification in other aspects of life
(12)	Criminal history	Index of impulse control and overall functioning, sex crimes signal increased risk for sexual abuse, index of superego functioning.
(13)	Sexual abuse	Possible confession or other incriminating statements, to blame victim, level of responsibility taken for the abuse

Source: Faller (1993)

Figure 3.3 Interview data gathered from the abuser

Much has been published about the assessment of child abusers and rapists. Little has been published however regarding the assessment of exhibitionism and exhibitionists. Nevertheless the general classes of interview data described above for child sexual abuse can be extrapolated to other sexually abusive behaviour including exhibitionism. Concerning a more detailed examination of exhibitionism we recommend that the following questions are addressed:

- **Who is exposed to?** Children (male/female/both), adolescents, adults elderly? Some or all of these?
- **Where does exposure occur?** e.g. from bedroom windows, in a car, on public transport, in parks etc?
- **When does exposure occur?** e.g. is there a set pattern (always late at night) or is this an apparently random/opportunistic activity?
- **What is involved in the act?** e.g. does the perpetrator talk to the victim, how is the victim 'groomed', how is the victim's attention caught, is masturbation involved, if so is this to ejaculation, what does the perpetrator wear during the act?
- **How many victims are involved in each episode?**
- **How long is each exhibitionist episode?** e.g. will the perpetrator move site and re-victimise others?
- **How does the exhibitionist prepare for the acts?**
- **What are common antecedents and consequences of offending?**

- **What fantasies does the perpetrator use during the commission of the act?**
- **What explanation does the perpetrator offer for his behaviour?**
- **What is the frequency of exposure?** What is the longest period the exhibitionist has gone between episodes?
- **What is the natural history of the problem?** How old was the client when fantasies of the act occurred, when did exposure first occur, when was it first detected, etc?
- **How many exhibitionist acts does the client estimate he has committed?**
- **What other paraphilias are evident?** e.g. transvestism, sadism, voyeurism, prowling/shadowing, obscene phone calling, frottage, burglary (motivated by a desire to frighten the victim and 'intrude')?
- **What is the typical victim reaction reported by the perpetrator?**
- **Can the perpetrator describe what is arousing/reinforcing in respect of the victim's reaction?** e.g. is the perpetrator aroused by the victim's fear, surprise, disgust?

Often one of the most worrying aspects of exhibitionism for workers is that of whether the behaviour will progress to 'hands on' sexual assault. Crucial to addressing this question is the determination of the **pattern** of the exhibitionistic behaviour. We should never assume exhibitionism to be a trivial nuisance act and should remember those clients who have sexually assaulted adults whose behaviour began with a pattern of exhibitionism in their earlier development.

To determine the pattern to exhibitionistic behaviour we advise the following are determined:

- Does the behaviour occur infrequently but of a more aggressive character or has it stabilised in frequency and intensity?
- Is the behaviour increasingly characterised by greater impulsivity and risk taking, e.g. with respect to the likelihood of detection or the act being witnessed?
- Does the behaviour reflect the shadowing of victims and attempts to engage them in sexual talk and pseudo-sexual behaviour?
- Does the behaviour follow increasingly sadistic sexual fantasy associated with the exhibitionist act?
- Does the behaviour leave the abuser feeling frustrated and angry?
- Does the abuser report anger, revenge, or control as a motive for the behaviour?

As can be seen from the above, one of the most crucial aspects of sex abuser evaluation will be a rigorous analysis of not only the 'index offence', but also preceding abusive behaviours. We recommend that to achieve this, a functional analysis of the relationship between abusive behaviour, the antecedent events and post abuse consequences be undertaken. Perkins (1991) has outlined this process and we support and recommend its use.

Perkins suggests that the abuser's deviant behaviour should be examined alongside preceding events (antecedents) as well as their consequences. He adds that this can be done at different levels of the abuser's functioning and refers to Lazarus' (1976) concept of multi-modal analysis. Following this modal we have found it most useful in practice to separate the immediate (proximal) and less immediate (distal) antecedents across the domains of the abusers thoughts, feelings and fantasies, as well as behaviour, in effect gathering information to complete the outline below.

	Distal Antecedent Events	Proximal Antecedent Events	Abuse Behaviour	Consequences
Behaviour				
Thoughts				
Feelings				
Fantasies				

When asking questions of each part of the matrix we have found it most useful to work left to right across one domain. For example, the client is asked to describe in detail what he **did** in the days prior to the abuse, followed by the day itself, including a detailed description of the minutes prior to the abuse being perpetrated. The abuse itself is then described in terms of what the abuser did, followed by what the abuser did in the moments, minutes and hours subsequent. The same stages are then described again by the client, this time focusing on what the client was **thinking** during these various stages. The questioning is repeated to ask the client his **feelings** at each stage, followed finally by assessment of the **fantasies** the client might have had throughout.

It should be noted that to undertake such an analysis thoroughly will take time. It is rare in our experience for an abusive act to be analysed using such a procedure in less than two hours. An emerging theme throughout this text will be that of the time necessary to undertake a rigorous assessment of any client. Inadequate evaluation is likely to lead to inadequate decision making. In this field this can be dangerous for all concerned. For those service managers reading this text the message is clear. Assessment is not a superficial activity, resources have to be allocated properly.

A model which complements that described above to assist in asking questions about the sequence of events leading through the abuse has been described by McGuire and Priestley (1985) – the 5W-H Model. The letters here stand for who, what, why, where, when and how? The repeated use of these simple questions (de-emphasising the 'why' question, as many clients have little understanding of causation or might be tempted to speculate inappropriately) is often helpful in the situational analysis of an abusive act.

There are various tips which might be considered to reflect good interviewing practice. Morrison and Print (1995) have summarised these for adolescent clients (reflecting on the motivational interviewing work of Miller and Rollnick (1991)). These are adapted below as a list of 'things to do and things to avoid' when interviewing. The suggestions are also based on feedback from those we have trained.

The 'Do's' of Interviewing
Before the interview:
- Plan the objectives of the interview beforehand.
- Familiarise yourself with background information.
- Be aware of the diversity of human sexuality – a knowledge base is important.
- Practice interviewing, co-interviewing styles and tactics with a supervisor or consultant.
- Ensure that a comfortable and secure environment is available for the interview.

During the interview:
- At the beginning of the interview be clear about the limits of confidentiality described above.
- Acknowledge the client's anxiety and use this acknowledgement to help motivate the client.
- Respect the client as having the capacity to change.
- Be prepared to go into details.
- Be flexible.
- Be patient.
- Stand back from the interview if you get stuck.
- Ask 'when' and 'how' questions.
- Check that the client understands the questions – paraphrase and summarise regularly.
- Reinforce the client's openness.
- Control the interview and structure the interview – avoid side tracking and distractions.
- Try and stay objective.
- Don't try to do too many things at once.
- Record important issues as they arise, especially those that cannot be dealt with at that moment.
- Encourage honesty.
- Say if you don't understand something.

- Don't be afraid of silence.
- Register scepticism.
- Take care of yourself – note what upsets you, angers you, or arouses you, and talk about it afterwards.
- Remember that hypothetical questions can be useful.
- Asking the client to rate feelings and emotions can be useful.
- Always remember why you are conducting the interview – don't get distracted.

The process of the interview will be assisted greatly if the interviewer opens the interview skilfully. The 'openers' are standard for any interview situation:

- Ensure that proper introductions are made.
- Check out the client's understanding of the purpose of the interview.
- Explain any note taking or recording to be used.
- Explain the limits of confidentiality.
- Explain the duration of the interview and ensure the client is clear as to what will happen following the interview.

Things to avoid during interviewing:

- Avoid asking the 'why' question too frequently.
- Don't ask long, complicated questions, full of hidden meaning.
- Don't start to give the client therapy during an assessment interview – first understand the client before trying to change the client.
- Don't use words the client doesn't understand.
- Don't bully the client.
- Don't rush to understand the client – don't be seduced by apparently simple models explaining offending and offences.
- Don't interview the client if you can't give the client proper attention and care.

Workers are often uneasy as to the detail and depth of questioning demanded in this work. We would argue that there are many reasons for interviewing sexual abusers in depth. These include:

- to build a complete, multi-factorial profile of the abuse and the abuser
- to help generate hypotheses about why the abuse occurred (i.e. using the interview to prompt, as well as confirm, hypotheses)
- to establish a firm basis for intervention, particularly when dealing with issues of sexual arousal, sexual fantasy and emotional satisfaction

- to demonstrate to the abuser that the interviewer is competent and confident, i.e. a tactical strategy to show that the interviewer 'knows' his/her subject
- to establish a clear baseline of information against which future attitudes and statements can be gauged (this is particularly useful when dealing with denial strategies)
- the abuser expects to be interviewed in depth – not to do so might model minimisation or avoidance
- to establish or maintain the interviewer in a position of control
- to check on previous information obtained from/about the abuser, i.e. to avoid using misleading or misinformed opinion
- to expose the abuser's attitudes towards his/her abusing, in particular to expose issues of denial, rationalisation and minimisation.

In our training of staff who work to develop their assessment skills we have identified common errors made in interviewing sexual abusers. We conclude this section on interviewing by offering examples of them:

- inaccurate paraphrasing, which may model denial or minimisation:

  > e.g. Abuser: 'I got Rosemary to touch me.'
  > Worker: 'So Rosemary touched you.'

- accepting one fact or explanation without pursuing other possibilities:

  > e.g. finding out that a client has buggered a victim without pursuing explanations of that behaviour (such as a coprophilia, sadism, 'faceless sex')

- not interviewing the client in depth:

  > e.g. finding that a client has buggered a victim, but not finding out how victim compliance was achieved.

- offering implicit therapy or premature hypotheses to clients within the assessment interview:

  > e.g. Worker: 'I guess it was difficult for you to build relationships with people of your own age, given your tragic upbringing.'

- using words or phrases a client may not understand:

  > e.g. Worker: 'I guess you crossed a double taboo in your abuse of that boy.'
  > Worker: 'Empathy for victims is sometimes hard to achieve.'

- not sticking with a line of enquiry – ie. getting diverted.

QUESTIONNAIRES AND RATING SCALES

Oliver and Chambers (1993) reviewed self-report measures used in sexual aggression research. They highlighted Hall's (1990) finding that equivocal relationships had been found in general between measures such as personality inventories, sexual activity and interest surveys and attitudes about women scales on the one hand, and sexually aggressive behaviour on the other. Social desirability as well as the abuser's distorted view of his behaviour is suggested to limit the validity of information gained from such self report measures.

Nevertheless the use of questionnaire methods to gather information about clients is likely to continue, not least as such methods assist in gathering information in a systematic and structured way and are useful in prompting the questioning of specific attitudes and behaviours which might be overlooked in the clinical interview. Indeed, such is the use of these methods that Prentky and Edmunds (1997) have dedicated a text to the retrieval of several inventories, scales and questionnaires. In Part III of this text we have tried to indicate sources of other materials to complement the materials gathered by Prentky and Edmunds.

As Prentky and Edmunds note:

(1) Very few questionnaires and inventories have any normative/data on sex offenders.

(2) Very few have been validated on samples of sexual offenders.

(3) Many have unknown psychometric properties (for example we don't know how reliable they are or whether they really measure what they suggest they do).

(4) There is a distinction to be drawn between 'clinical assessment' and 'risk assessment'. They argue that risk assessment requires knowledge of the risk assessment literature, knowledge of the 'technical' aspects of prediction, and an awareness of how to distinguish or describe both low or high risk within the sex offender populations. We will return to this subject of risk assessment in Chapter Fourteen.

For those workers who are charged with responsibility for working with not only the abuser or alleged abuser of child sexual abuse but also the non abusing partner and/or victims a text by Cavanagh Johnson (1997) might be of special interest. Her 'child sexuality curriculum' for abused children and their parents has sections each built to deal with crucial issues for parents and children of abused families (i.e. sections on sexual values, sexual knowledge, communication about sex or sexuality, sexual abuse, boundaries, or children's sexual behaviours).

The curriculum is not targeted at therapy for the sex offender. However the curriculum is a rich source of questionnaires, exercises and knowledge quizzes which will be of general interest.

In our training of staff we have developed exercises to help delegates review the advantages and disadvantages of the use of questionnaire methods in the assessment of sexual abusers. The usual responses of delegates can be summarised as follows:

The 'pros' of questionnaire methods:

- They can be used as part of a structured interview.
- It is easier for some people to write about how they feel about sexual matters than talk about those feelings.
- Questionnaires can throw up or highlight inconsistencies in responses.
- Standardised measures can be developed.
- They can provide easy and standard measures reflecting change pre and post intervention.
- Following on from the above they can assist in evaluating interactions.
- They provide thinking time for the client.
- They ensure important things do not get missed.
- They can be very focused on the area of enquiry.

The 'cons' of questionnaire methods include:

- They might frighten clients.
- They are difficult to use with clients with literacy problems.
- They might be perceived as mechanical.
- Clients might be suspicious of their confidentiality.
- They might be construed of as a superficial, 'paper' exercise.
- They do not provide inherent, immediate feedback.
- Perhaps it is easier to fake good (or bad) such measures.
- They are open to ambiguity.

We believe questionnaire methods to have an important role to play in sexual abuser evaluations though urge practitioners to use such methods in conjunction with other methods, never in isolation. Again the practitioner has to bear in mind:

- what am I attempting to assess here?
- why am I attempting to assess this factor?
- what is the relevance and strength of the assessment tool or method I am using in this evaluation?

It is beyond the scope of this book to provide a critical description of all questionnaire materials applicable to sexual abuser evaluations. Chapters in Part III of this book list, within the measures sections, further information as to the range of materials available. Again, it should be stressed that such materials should be used with care.

An example of the level of criticism such tools have received is served by the Multiphasic Sex Inventory (Nichols and Molinder 1984, Earle *et al.* 1995).

This instrument has gained popularity in the UK and has been pivotal in some research programmes. Earle *et al*. acknowledge its use in eliciting information, and report the MSI having as one of its primary aims those behaviours associated with rape and child abuse. The MSI is criticised however as being based on a model of chauvinistic or sexist sexuality, the test items of which not clearly distinguishing levels of intimacy within adult sexual behaviour. Earle *et al*. believe the test reflects a view of non intimate sexuality as normal, and are suspicious that accepting such non intimate arousal as normal reflects an 'objectified, dehumanised attitude toward women'. Earle *et al*. also criticise the test's questions, particularly on the obsessions scale, which are set in both the past and present tense, and which have confused some of their clients.

PENILE PLETHYSMOGRAPHIC ASSESSMENT

Commonly referred to as PPG assessment, this represents an attempt to undertake an objective assessment of sexual arousal. Penile responses are measured or recorded as a function of the client's exposure to sexually explicit materials, commonly slides depicting naked human forms, adult and child, male and female. Video tapes of sexually explicit scenes, commonly scenes including consenting and non-consenting sexual acts are also used. Less commonly, audio taped descriptions of sexual scenes might be used as stimulus material.

It is beyond the scope of this book to present a detailed critique of such phallometric assessment or indeed guidance as to how such measurements should be undertaken. Penile plethysmography is an intrusive and technologically demanding technique for which proper training, not only in the administration of materials, but also in their interpretation is necessary.

There is considerable debate as to the ethics of PPG assessment and concerns as to both the reliability and validity of the procedure. Some individuals are capable of suppressing arousal to stimulus materials which they find inherently arousing, some appear to be able to simulate arousal through non-arousing stimuli, for example, by using mental images whilst viewing non-arousing stimuli, of preferred sexual stimuli (Briggs 1979).

It is our belief that PPG assessments are best used as bio feedback devices for motivated clients undergoing treatment who wish to learn ways of controlling sexual arousal or discerning early stages of arousal. We would not advise its use as a 'lie detector', i.e. as the sole indicator of deviant sexual interest in clients who would deny such.

PROJECTIVE TESTING

The essence of projective testing is the interpretation of the client's wishes, desires and understanding of events from their descriptions of apparently ambiguous materials. Typically the client is presented with a picture and asked to describe it or construct a narrative or explanation of what is seen. The tester assumes that what the client says is a projection of the client's unconscious, or part revealed desires, attitudes or needs. Such tests are often perceived as representing psychiatry and psychology at their most mysterious.

Problems have beset the use of projective tests for many years. It is often difficult for different testers to achieve agreement as to the content of client's descriptions of materials. Some aspects of projective descriptions might not 'capture' known behavioural traits.

Similarly, descriptions drawn from projective interpretations might match some though not all known traits. Cronbach (1969) in his seminal tome *Essentials of Psychological Testing* commented '...projective techniques as currently interpreted are not dependable sources of complex descriptions, although some reports are appreciably better than random guesses. Their value can be improved with further development of scoring reliability and interpretative theory.' The challenge of this comment, although now dated, is still relevant.

It is interesting to note the recent publication of a set of projective materials for work with sexual abusers – the Sexual Projective Card Set (SPCS) (Card. R 1996, Behavioural Technology Inc). The test is described as 'a projective paper and pencil test especially developed to sample themes from a client's life to sexual issues.' Charcoal drawings were developed on the basis of themes provided by clinicians experienced in treating adult and adolescent sexual abusers and victims. Five categories of drawing are provided covering normal and faulty sexual development, sexual offender issues, paraphilia and victim issues. The drawings were 'designed to permit either a normal or deviant projection'. The publisher has suggested clinical and research uses for the materials but is keen to stress that no validity studies have been completed or published yet.

> 'In our limited use of the SPCS test with...sex offender populations, the SPCS stories produced may elicit responses consistent with power, control and manipulation dynamics of which the client may be unaware. Further stories may reveal a depth of deviant thoughts, feelings, defences and emotions not generally elicited by more structured tests...we are also developing an objective scoring system, but until such time as the data is available we recommend that the stories *not* be used in evaluations for determining guilt, dangerousness or a clients likelihood of recidivism.'

The SPCS provides an extension to our assessment repertoire though it is clear that given the comments above, considerable caution has to be exercised in the use of the materials. The danger lies in making assumptions about a client's motives and interests which are not valid. If the assessment of risk and pleas for treatment are based on faulty premises then not only is this potentially a waste of resources, but also dangerous. We recommend these materials be used only by those who have received training in projective testing and who understand the associated issues of discriminant validity and reliability.

BEHAVIOURAL OBSERVATIONS

Many workers become concerned when assessing sexual abusers that what their clients say might be different from what their clients think, feel and do. Indeed the phrases 'talk the talk' and 'walk the walk' have entered the vernacular to capture this dilemma. Observations of client's behaviour can add unique information to the overall assessment profile if the assessor is alert to this potential. It can be argued that whilst questionnaires can be faked, and whilst information can be presented in a distorted way during interview, observations of a client might give a truer picture of his motivation.

Observations can add particular information as to the client's motivation to cooperate and collaborate with the worker and the assessment process, it can assist in evaluations of the quality of inter personal relationships and it can raise issues of ongoing sexual attractions and grooming tactics.

Some very simple observations help us identify client's co-operation. Does the client arrive for sessions punctually? Is the client prepared for the sessions when he arrives? Has the client complied with homework requests between sessions? Is the client prepared to stay until the end of the sessions? Are there activities within the sessions which the client avoids?

It is very easy for the worker to underestimate the importance of these behaviours. We believe that this behaviour is a clue to client motivation. These behaviours we believe are associated with risk of relapse following treatment (Briggs and Lovelock 1991).

Much can be learned about the quality of the person's inter-personal relationships from observation. Let us consider the issue of domestic rape. We know of the association between domestic violence and rape within relationships (Campbell 1996). We also know of the power and control issues which are inherent within such relationships (Butts Stahly 1997). What can we learn of those clients who might have separated from their partners following allegations of domestic rape?

Crucial here are signs of ongoing use of power and control strategies; for example, if the couple have a child, and following separation when the client might have staying contact with his child, is the child collected from and delivered promptly to the victimised partner? Does the client break other rules of contact, for example collecting the child from school unscheduled? Does the client continue to use abuse and harassment in effect to punish the woman for leaving the relationship? Does the child become the focus of power and control struggles, for example with the client seeking sole custody of the child? Does the client honour financial agreements in respect of the child or former partner?

At a different level the nature of the client's relationship with the worker(s) can be very revealing. If the assessment is conducted on a co-working basis, does the client behave differently to one worker as opposed to the other? If so, what is the basis of this behaviour – is it the gender of the worker, their race, their perceived authority or status, or some other dynamic?

The client and worker, for better or worse, are in a relationship from the outset, each defining the parameters of their relationship from their own perspective, each wanting to ensure their needs are met in a safe and purposeful way which does not disturb their emotional equilibrium. Not surprisingly, the client within this relationship will attempt to influence the worker, and vice versa. The behaviour the client uses towards the worker often mimics the behaviour the client uses towards others, and on occasions can mimic the grooming process used in the abuse itself. The worker should be alert to the style of the client's interaction therefore, as well as the content of what they say.

Clients can often use 'seductive' strategies with workers, for example: 'you're the only person I have ever been able to tell this to'; 'you at least know what you're doing, 'so and so' hadn't a clue'; 'I guess your job must be really stressful, you must take care of yourself'. Alternatively, power and intimidation tactics can be brought into play, for example with the client attempting to bully the worker, or becoming hostile when asked questions about particular aspects of their behaviour.

What can the worker learn of the client's on-going sexual interests/attractions? The worker should be aware of the casual asides clients may make during interviews, for example asking the worker if he/she has children and any associated questions, such as referring to television programmes or other media which might give a clue to on-going attractions (particularly story lines the client may have enjoyed in soap operas, documentaries and the like). The client's non-verbal behaviour during assessment should be of note; for example how does the client scan his environment? It is surprising how many offices contain photographs of workers' children, have posters on the wall depicting children, have shared waiting areas in which children occasionally play – all this can be fantasy fodder for a child abuser.

A rich source of information about clients, their lifestyle and relationships is to be gained from observing clients in their home environment. Unfortunately both for reasons of cost and safety many professions have restricted home based assessments. There is an argument however that this leads to valuable information being missed.

It is always interesting to note how the abuser or alleged abuser interacts with other adults and children within the home, to note who is visiting the home and why, and to gain an impression of lifestyle in respect to stressors apparent in the home environment. Without wishing to play detective there are also advantages to be gained from visiting the client's home in terms of attempting to assess whether there are paraphernalia or materials which might support fetishistic interests underlining offending behaviour. In conducting a recent 'risk assessment' of a man who had allegedly taken indecent photographs of children, upon visiting his home there were numerous photographs of children in swimming costumes and leotards on the walls, there were school girl annuals on the bookshelves (the man had no children) and there were binoculars on a window ledge of a window facing a local park where children played.

There is a word of warning to be given about observation. The workers observing have to be aware that they might see what they want to see rather than what has occurred. Therefore it is important that behaviour is recorded accurately, that what is said is recorded verbatim, that the sequence of events is accurately described with chronology clear, that alternative explanations for the behaviour being observed are put forward, and that special consideration be given to the impact of observations on the 'naturalness' of the behaviour being observed (in other words simply being observed will make many clients behave in ways that are not natural to them).

For those assessing clients for civil courts and family proceedings particularly where issues of risk are to be inferred in part from the quality of contact the abuser might have with a child, we would stress the necessity of keeping very detailed and adequate records of observations and with clear timings being recorded of events throughout the contact session, for example with five minute markers being recorded on the page.

OTHER APPROACHES

To fail to prepare is to prepare to fail! This is particularly so in the assessment of sexual abusers. We recommend that before the client is seen for the first time that all relevant case papers are read. Cumming and Buell (1977) highlight this point in their advice to probation officers preparing pre-sentence reports.

They highlight that documentary review enables the worker:

- to learn of the detail of the abuser's history, particularly those aspects the client may choose to omit or gloss over during the interview. (This in turn might help the worker plan a strategy for dealing with such denial and rationalisation.)
- to update on investigations conducted since the preliminary disclosure
- to learn of eye witness accounts of the acts – often the victim statement is the only such account
- to read into the abuser's statement and learn of patterns of denial or admission, and the abuser's attitudes towards his victims
- to learn from papers concerning previous offences whether there is a discernible pattern to the deviant behaviour, whether there is escalation, and the risks taken in abusing
- to learn from records of periods of past supervision or treatment the behaviour and attitudes of the client under supervision.

ASSESSMENT OF CLIENTS WITH LEARNING DISABILITIES

For those clients with learning disabilities we would recommend that assessment include an evaluation of cognitive functioning. By this we mean that the client's intellectual, memory, attention/concentration, perception and language skills be assessed. Such an assessment will help address issues pertaining to the client's likely rate and style of learning and their ability to understand and remember essential messages of therapy. It will inform how best to work with the client and could help explain apparently inconsistent or incongruent behaviours. In addition, it is desirable for cognitive assessment to include evaluation of the client's literacy skills, not only word recognition skills as indicated by traditional reading screening tests, but also reading comprehension skills. Such testing will inevitably include the services of a suitably qualified psychologist, normally within the UK a chartered clinical or educational psychologist with expertise in this area.

Notwithstanding the above, many of the techniques already described, particularly the interview, behavioural observation and documentary analysis will apply to clients with learning disabilities.

Little has been written about work with learning disabled sexual abusers, that is, in comparison with publications about non-disabled adult or adolescent abusers. Nolley, Muccigrosso and Zignan (1996) describe a treatment programme for eight clients with primarily mild or moderate learning difficulties, and refer to the assessments used with this group. A multi-level assessment is described, including:

- information gathered from case management agency files, significant others and police reports

- 'clinical assessment' including periodic interviews with parents, siblings and other family, professional group home supervisors, vocational training supervisors and independent living skills supervisors

- direct observation and personal interview during sessions, including sessions conducted in the client's home

- self reports of social skills and role playing exercises to highlight social skills deficits

- interviews and interventions to assess knowledge of culturally acceptable behaviour

- intellectual assessment and adaptive behavioural milestones to 'establish or verify mental disability'.

Interestingly, the authors declined to use penile plethysmography with their clients, arguing that 'integrity of consent may be questionable'. Similarly they did not use structured assessments of sexual history and behaviour at the outset of the programme as they believed that their subjects 'might fabricate answers to intrusive questions early in education/treatment'.

Two structured assessment tests are referred to by the authors, the *Life Facts: Sexuality Questionnaire* (Stanfield, 1990) and the *Woodvale Sexuality Assessment* (1989)

For further information on the subject of learning disabled sexual offenders the reader is referred to the work of James Haven, and Haven *et al.*'s (1990) text in particular.

CHAPTER FOUR

Contexts for Assessment

Assessment is an integral part of all work with sexual abusers and should be a continuous process at every stage of that work. There are however several contexts within which assessments are required for specific purposes and these are the focus of this chapter.

- Civil Proceedings
- Child Protection Conferences
- Mental Health
- Hostels
- Pre-Sentence Reports
- Prisoner Release Considerations
- 'Schedule One' Offences

The contextual requirements of each of these areas is outlined with references for more detailed reading where appropriate, and the specific implications in relation to sexual abusers is then discussed. Readers are invited to make selective use of this chapter, referring to whichever areas are relevant to their own practice.

CIVIL PROCEEDINGS

Assessments of abusers and alleged abusers are often called upon in civil proceedings where matters of child care, contact and supervision are to be determined.

Under the Children Act 1989 the general principles that are to be applied in Court proceedings are set out. The child's welfare is paramount, be that with respect to decision making about the child's upbringing, the administration of the child's property, the progress of hearings, or indeed as to whether or not an order is made.

The 1989 Act introduces a checklist of relevant factors to be regarded by the Courts in all applications relating to local authority care and supervision of children. This checklist is as follows:

'a court shall have regard in particular to –

(a) the ascertainable wishes and feelings of the child concerned (considered in the light of his age and understanding)

(b) his physical, emotional and educational needs

(c) the likely effect on him of any change in his circumstances

(d) his age, sex, background and any characteristics of his which the Court considers relevant

(e) any harm which he has suffered or is at risk of suffering

(f) how capable each of his parents and any other person in relation to whom the Court considers the question to be relevant is of meeting his needs

(g) the range of powers available to the Court under this act in the proceedings in question.'

Clearly this welfare checklist is of immediate relevance to those engaged in offering opinions to the Court as to the risk of any individual abusing a child, in whatever way, and as evidenced by items (e) and (f).

If the Court is to protect any child at risk of harm via the imposition of Care or Supervision Orders the Court must be satisfied

'(a) that the child concerned is suffering, or is likely to suffer, significant harm, **and**

(b) that the harm or likelihood of harm, is attributable to –

(i) the care given to the child, or likely to be given to him if the order were not made, not being what it would be reasonable to expect a parent to give him; or

(ii) the child's being beyond parental control.'

Similarly, if an Emergency Protection Order is to be made the Court must be satisfied that there is reasonable cause to believe that the child is likely to suffer significant harm if that child is not removed to accommodation provided on or behalf of the applicant, or does not remain in the place where he is being accommodated. Implicit therefore in the Act is a framework which should assist those engaged in assessing abusers and suspected abusers. The focus of assessment is to determine evidence of the likelihood of harm as a function of the abuser's behaviour or likely behaviour. In the 'Directions' given to those undertaking such assessments the phrase 'Risk Assessment' is often used to summarise what is called for here in respect of the assessment process. Such assessments are often requested alongside other investigations, for example for an assessment of the non-abusing partner's ability to protect', the likely validity of any allegations made and so forth. Chapter Fourteen of this book will comment in more detail on 'Risk Assessment'.

House of Lords Ruling

In assessing abusers and alleged abusers in civil proceedings workers will need to take account of a recent House of Lords judgement which clarifies some definitions and addresses issues in relation to the burden of proof. In the case of Re H a man Mr R was married to Mrs R. There were four children, all girls. D1 and D2 were daughters of Mrs R's previous marriage to Mr H; D3 and D4 were daughter's of Mr and Mrs R's marriage. Mr R was alleged to have raped D1 but was acquitted by the Crown Court on all counts. The local authority continued with their application for a Care Order based on the same allegations, asking the Civil Courts to find that the events had occurred, the burden of proof in the Civil Courts being 'the balance of probabilities' and therefore lower than that in the Criminal Courts, i.e. 'beyond reasonable doubt.'

The House of Lords (Re H All England Law reports 3.1.96) found against the authority. The following findings emerge from the ruling which may influence cases in future.

- The standard of proof in care proceedings is confirmed as being the balance of probabilities, but it is asserted that

    (1)   Conclusions must be based on facts and not just suspicion.
    (2)   The burden of proof lays clearly on the applicant (i.e. the local authority).

- The phrase 'likely to suffer significant harm' is defined as meaning that 'there is a real possibility that the child would suffer significant harm'.

- The more serious or improbable the allegation of abuse, the more convincing is the evidence required to prove it.

Some social workers have observed that this judgement will make it more difficult to secure orders to protect children, where there are concerns which are difficult to prove to a high standard. Lawyers commenting after the case asserted that equally it would protect children who may be removed from the home unnecessarily on the basis of poor evidence. Richard White (1996) comments that the judgement may achieve the 'bizarre result that the more serious the allegation, the more difficult it becomes for the local authority to satisfy the criteria and protect the child'.

Whichever view is taken, it is right to say that the Re H judgement clarifies a number of issues. White believes it may reduce the number of cases brought before the Court and be regarded as part of a move towards working in partnership with parents. It may be difficult to provide services to a child where harm is neither accepted nor proved. The decision emphasises the need for cogent and coherent argument and White advises against focusing on single issues.

Family Courts

For those practitioners who are called upon to evaluate alleged abusers in divorce and Residence/Contact disputes the so called 'clinical research approach' is recommended. Assessment here is summarised as a process by Ehrenberg and Elterman (1995)

(1) The assessment should be approached with professional knowledge and skills; the assessment should be updated on an ongoing basis and documented in the final report.

(2) The assessor's role should be clearly identified, and the assessment process should be described verbally and in writing to those involved, including the time frame and the names of those who will receive copies of the final report.

(3) As much relevant data as possible should be collected through multiple assessment techniques (e.g. interviewing, observation, testing) from as many sources as possible (relevant family members, key individuals, previous or current evaluators/investigators/therapists) while noting missing or insufficient data and why these data could not be obtained.

(4) Multiple hypotheses or possible explanations for the allegations under evaluation should be raised and then thoroughly explored.

(5) Any data that are consistent or inconsistent with any of the hypothesis should be documented and explained.

(6) Subsequently the assessment data should be integrated to conclude whether the child's and parents' and/or third parties' behaviours and psychological functioning are consistent with, inconsistent with, or inconclusive regarding the sexual abuse allegation.

(7) It will be on the basis of the above that specific recommendations about custody and visitation will be made bearing in mind the child's needs, interests, and primarily safety.

CHILD PROTECTION CONFERENCE

The Child Protection Conference (often loosely referred to as a Case Conference) epitomises two central tenets of assessment in child protection i.e. that assessment should be an inter agency, interdisciplinary function, and that assessments should be subject to constant review. Conferences are organised under Area Protection Committee procedures and detailed guidance on their functioning is given in the Government's guide to the 1989 Children Act called *Working Together* (Home Office *et al.* 1991). The language of *Working Together* constantly reiterates the importance of the Child Protection Conference describing it as 'central to child protection procedures' and the 'prime forum' for sharing of information. If the local authority Social Services Department (or the National Society for Prevention of Cruelty to Children acting in their stead) receives information indicating that a child may be at risk it should convene a conference of all relevant professionals, the parents of the child, and if appropriate, the child itself.

The conference is not a quasi-judicial hearing and is not convened to decide matters of fact (notably whether or not a given alleged incident of abuse has occurred or not). These can only be decided by a court. Indeed the *only* decision a conference can make is whether a child should be put on the child protection register, or if it is already on whether it should remain on. If a child is so 'registered' a child protection plan should be drawn up with individuals assigned to undertake each aspect of the plan, and a key worker (from the local authority) identified to co-ordinate the plan.

Child protection conferences take two forms:

(1) The Initial Child Protection Conference. This is called as soon as possible after referral and after an investigation has been undertaken under Section 47 of the Children Act. This should be within eight working days.

(2) The Child Protection Review. If a child is placed on the register the case must be reviewed at least every six months to examine whether or not registration should continue.

Section 6.39 of *Working Together* identifies the Requirements for Registration as follows.

'Before a child is registered the conference must decide that there is, or is a likelihood of, significant harm leading to the need for a child protection plan. One of the following requirements needs to be satisfied:

(i) There must be one or more identifiable incidents which can be described as having adversely affected the child. They may be acts of commission or omission. They can be either physical, sexual, emotional or neglectful. It is important to identify a specific occasion or occasions when the incident has occurred. Professional judgement is that further incidents are likely:

or

(ii) Significant harm is expected on the basis of professional judgement of findings of the investigation in this individual case or on research evidence.

The conference will need to establish so far as they can a cause of the harm or likelihood of harm. This cause could also be applied to siblings or other children living in the same household so as to justify registration of them. Such children should be categorised according to the area of concern.'

To register under the category of sexual abuse the conference must be satisfied that there is

'actual or likely sexual exploitation of a child or adolescent. The child may be dependent and/or developmentally immature'.

Areas of concern may overlap. Sexual abuse may result in physical injury and include facets of neglect or emotional abuse. However conferences should not register in different categories as a 'catch all' nor exaggerate concerns in order to register as a means to access resources. In some cases there may be sufficient concern to register a child before it is born.

De-registration can only occur when members of a review conference agree that the concerns are no longer present at a level to warrant continued registration. This would apply if a child and family had moved permanently to another area and that area accepted responsibility for the case, if the child ceased to become a child in law, or if the child died. A more complex reason for de-registration would be that 'the original factors which led to registration no longer apply'. Considerations would include work done with the family during the protection plan, the child or abusing adult no longer having contact, or after completion of a comprehensive assessment, a detailed analysis of risk showing that registration is not necessary.

As in all child care practice, the welfare of the child is paramount, but an important principle of the Children Act is that problems are addressed in partnership with parents. However if the interests of parents and children are at odds it is clear that the children's welfare comes first. Consequently the Chair of the conference may need to make a decision to exclude one or both parents. Exclusions should be kept to a minimum to the extent that being the alleged abuser does not of itself debar a parent.

The Chair of the conference should be independent of the case. Other professionals are urged to prepare properly for conferences and provide written reports if relevant. Attenders to the conference should give full information and be clear about what is fact, observation, allegation or opinion. Each should be clear about what is expected of them as a result of the protection plan and about any aspects of the discussions and decisions about which they disagree.

Dissenting views should be minuted. Professionals responsible for undertaking aspects of the protection plan are likely to meet between conferences to plan their work and share information.

Whilst Child Protection Conferences are only empowered to decide on the issue of registration they frequently make recommendations about actions which agencies might undertake. However it is for the agencies to decide whether to pursue that action. Notable in this context are decisions about prosecution of alleged perpetrators of abuse by the Police and Crown Prosecution Service, or Civil Proceedings by the Local Authority. Professionals attending conferences should be clear about the level at which they can agree to take action on behalf of their own agencies.

Working Together recommends joint training of agencies to enhance the skills, knowledge and judgement of staff in this field. It is critically important that all workers have a shared understanding of the nature of child abuse and of the roles of each of the agencies involved. However there are other issues which may inhibit the proper functioning of inter-agency systems and it is helpful for workers to be alert to these in order to avoid pitfalls. Many of these issues were identified during the Cleveland Inquiry (Butler-Schloss 1987) and whilst generally matters have improved markedly since then our experiences would suggest that they have not been resolved entirely in every area.

Tensions may exist about the role of an enquiry. For instance if the purpose of a medical examination is perceived by one professional as essentially to gather evidence and by another as protecting the health of a child, then approaches may be very different. Value systems or theoretical perspectives about the nature of sexual (or other) abuse may be markedly different. It is essential that this does not cause professionals to be dogmatic in defending their position and that information and opinions are shared and considered in a balanced manner.

Lack of clarity about the roles of agencies represented can cause difficulties. Whilst agencies have a right to make their own decisions, it would be a sign that the Area Child Protection Committee was seriously malfunctioning if agencies were persistently ignoring the recommendations of conferences. Political wranglings between agencies should not be allowed to intrude into discussions. At a practitioner level the failure to understand roles can cause problems. For example a common feeling amongst colleagues in the Probation Service is that, if they indicate that a probation order may be a sensible outcome for an abuser, they are sometimes perceived as advocates for the offender when other professionals feel that an apparently more punitive response would be more appropriate.

Informal alliances can skew discussions within conferences. These may include personal friendships between professionals, or a sense of cliquishness may exist amongst workers who associate together frequently, which may intimidate others from commenting fully. It is important that workers stand aside from these personal or professional alliances. Other interpersonal issues relate to the status of workers.

There may be disproportionate weight given to the opinion of some professionals because of their qualifications or status, when someone such as a foster-parent who sees a child for many hours per day may have a huge amount of very relevant and important information. It is important that all information and opinions are heard, assessed and considered carefully and dispassionately.

MENTAL HEALTH AND THE MENTAL HEALTH ACT 1983

The Mental Health Act (1983) makes provision for the care of mentally disordered patients. Mental disorder, within the act, 'means mental illness, arrested or incomplete development of mind, psychopathic disorder and any other disorder or disability of mind...' Importantly for those known to have sexually abused others, 'nothing...shall be construed as implying that a person may be dealt with under this Act as suffering from mental disorder or from any form of mental disorder...by reason only of promiscuity or other immoral conduct, sexual deviancy, or dependence on alcohol and drugs'. Therefore having committed or expressed interest in sexually abusive behaviours is insufficient to warrant an individual being dealt with by the Act.

We mention the Mental Health Act within this chapter to indicate the special requirements in assessing sexual abusers who suffer serious mental health problems. It is beyond the scope of the chapter to describe in detail the Act, and readers are referred to Jones 1996 for a recent and detailed review of the Act. There are however some parts we would wish to highlight.

Part 3 of the 1983 Mental Health Act deals with patients concerned with criminal proceedings. Within the framework of the Act, any assessment of the person is a medical responsibility. That is not to say, however, that appropriate members of the clinical team who might be expected to play a role in the person's care and treatment should not be involved. For example, doctors are advised to make contact with the social worker or probation officer preparing pre-sentence reports, especially where psychiatric treatment is suggested as a condition of a probation order.

Approved social workers (social workers with recognised special training in this area) and doctors are encouraged to recognise their specific roles in assessment. In the revised Code of Practice which was drafted to support the administration of the Act, advice is given as to good practice in the assessment of those persons with mental health problems where assessment may lead to an application for admission to hospital under the Mental Health Act.

- Doctors and approved social workers should arrive at their own independent decisions.
- The work should be underpinned by good working relationships based on knowledge and responsibilities.
- Assessment should be carried out jointly unless good reasons prevent it.
- An agreement should be reached between the professionals involved in the assessment process as to how their responsibilities can best be discharged.

Guidance is also given as to factors to be taken into account when assessing a patient for compulsory hospital admission. For this to occur the person must not only suffer a mental disorder as defined by the Act, but the admission must be proven to be necessary in the interests of his own health, *or* the interests of his own safety, *or* for the protection of other people. Those involved in assessing patients for compulsory admission are encouraged, via the code of practice, to consider:

- the patient's wishes and view of his own needs
- his social and family circumstances
- the risk of making assumptions based on a person's sex, social and cultural background or ethnic origin
- the possibility of misunderstandings which may be caused by other medical/health conditions including deafness
- the nature of the illness/behaviour disorder
- what may be known about the patient by his nearest relatives, any other relatives or friends and professionals involved, assessing in particular how reliable this information is
- other forms of care or treatment including, when relevant, consideration of whether the patient would be willing to accept medical treatment in hospital informally or as an out-patient
- the needs of the patient, family or others with whom the patient lives
- the need for others to be protected from the patient

- the impact that compulsory admission would have on the patient's life after discharge from detention.

For those sexual abusers who are 'restricted patients' (where the Court has imposed powers to restrict the patient's discharge from hospital to protect the public from serious harm) the Mental Health Act specifies special responsibilities for the Secretary of State in the management and oversight of such 'restricted patients'. The Home Office routinely consider cases of restricted patients, inviting the multi-disciplinary team caring for the client to indicate why the patient had been dangerous in the past, whether the patient is still dangerous (and if so, why? If not, why not? And in what circumstances they might be dangerous again), and what the treatment plan is.

All cases are evaluated across a range of criteria, including an understanding of the factors underpinning the index offence and previous dangerous behaviour, what changes have occurred to affect the perceived level of dangerousness, the potential risk factors in the future (e.g. compliance with medication, substance abuse, potential future circumstances); the patient's current attitudes to the index offence, other dangerous behaviour and any previous victims; outward evidence of change including the patient's current attitude's to drugs and alcohol, where relevant.

For patients with dangerous sexual behaviour clinical teams are asked to consider

(1) whether the patient shows an undesirable interest in the victim type

(2) the patient's access to the victim type and the patient's attitude towards this group

(3) what form his sexual activity in hospital has taken

(4) what do psychological tests or other evaluation indicate?

(5) what is the current content of fantasy material?

HOSTELS

The management of approved probation and bail hostels is governed by the Probation Services' National Standard for the Supervision of Offenders in the Community (1995) and the Approved Probation and Bail Hostel Rules 1995. The National Standards state that

> 'The purpose of approved hostels is to provide an enhanced level of supervision to enable certain bailees and offenders to remain under supervision in the community. (They)…should be reserved for those who require this enhanced supervision and are not meant simply as accommodation. They should prove a supportive and structured environment within which their residents can be supervised effectively. But it should be clearly understood that approved hostels are **not secure** and so, unlike Prison Service establishments, cannot provide the same degree of protection from the risks posed by the most serious offenders.'

Despite the caveat in the last sentence above, hostels have a vital contribution to make in work with sexual abusers. They provide accommodation, support, and monitoring by trained staff. They offer an appropriate degree of care and control and aim to reduce the level of offending for those individuals for whom they have a statutory responsibility.

Many staff in hostels are trained in working with people in crisis and have a vital role to play in the assessment of offenders in the community.

> 'When offenders are placed in hostels this provides a particularly valuable setting in which to assess social problems, for example, a tendency towards social isolation, frequency of conflict and conflict resolution skills' (Beckett 1944). Probation Officers are required to confer with hostel staff when preparing presentence reports on those individuals who reside in hostels as it is recognized that 'hostel staff quickly acquire a body of knowledge about residents and become able to use this in making sound and balanced judgements.' (Home Office 1995)

When a client is bailed for assessment a key worker should be allocated. S(he) will prepare the bail assessment report assisted by other members of staff, addressing the client's motivation and willingness to address his problems. Hostel staff should ensure that residents comply with any bail conditions imposed by the Court. The police should be notified of any serious failures to comply with those conditions. Hostels have a curfew and failure to comply with that without reasonable excuse should be the subject of a formal warning, no more than two of which can be given before breach action is instigated.

Staff will identify areas in which they can help, such as with the improvement of social skills and self esteem, encouraging constructive activities, budgeting, relationship issues, alcohol or drug dependency, and will aim to provide support and practical assistance according to needs observed. Where violence is an issue, the safety of staff, residents and members of the community will be considered carefully.

Good practice requires that a meeting is held between the resident, the key worker and the probation officer or social worker to clarify expectations and to make decisions as to the appropriateness of a further period of residence at the hostel.

Residents in approved hostels after sentence either on probation or on supervision following release from custody are subject to the same enhanced supervision as with those on bail. Hostel staff have obligations to the local community and the assessment of risk will therefore be an ongoing consideration. That assessment should be based on good communication and joint work between the hostel staff and the supervising probation officer or social worker. Observations of the resident's behaviour, his interactions with other residents and members of staff, who he visits, what visits he receives, and how he spends his time can make a very valuable contribution to the assessment process. Those same observations will also contribute to assessment of sexual abusers' responses to any work taking place in respect of their offending behaviour.

Hostels and accommodation projects within the voluntary sector will be operating their own regimes but will also have much to offer in respect of work with sexual abusers. In all cases therefore every opportunity should be taken to make best use of the insight which accommodation staff can offer to the assessment process.

PRE SENTENCE REPORTS

A pre sentence report (PSR) is prepared for a criminal court by a probation officer (or local authority social worker) to assist the Court in determining the most suitable method of dealing with an offender (Home Office 1995). Whilst workers may wish to undertake full scale clinical assessments at this stage, time constraints may prevent this, and the content of reports should be guided by the relevant legal context in which the report is being presented. The reader's attention is specifically drawn to the Home Office's *National Standards for the Supervision of Offenders in the Community*, and the existence of sentencing guidelines and Appeal Court rulings referred to later.

A pre sentence report will usually be ordered by a court after conviction. In most areas administrative arrangements exist for the Probation Service to contact defendants after their committal to the Crown Court, prior to pleas being taken, in order to expedite progress at the Crown Court. At this stage a report should only be prepared with the consent of the defendant and after consulting his solicitor. It is essential to be clear about what exactly the defendant is willing to admit. If he is only admitting some of the allegations then reference should be made to local 'statements of preferred practice' (agreements between judges and the Probation Service) to ascertain whether a useful report can be prepared pre trial.

Subsequent to conviction a defendant's consent is not required for completion of a PSR. Indeed if he fails to co-operate with the preparation of the report the probation officer is still under a duty to report on the basis of what is known, for instance from Crown Prosecution papers or old records.

National Standards require that a PSR be impartial. McColl and Hargreaves (1993) identified a strong tendency for report writers in sex offender cases to present collusive reports in the face of spurious explanations by offenders. At the other extreme we have noted how workers' natural revulsion at the behaviour reported upon may manifest itself in very punitive language which is not evident in reports of other serious offences. Men who commit the most extreme offences are not always those who are most at risk of reoffending. The search for balance can be helped by proper support networks, co-working arrangements and quality control systems.

Pre sentence reports should address the following areas:

- offence analysis
- relevant information about the offender
- risk to the public of re-offending
- suitability of the offender to attend a community based programme (if relevant).

Before embarking on interviews with the defendant to address the above areas, report writers should ensure that they have prosecution documents, including victim statements, available along with previous departmental records if relevant. It is advisable to read these papers well in advance of the first interview as feelings of anger or disgust engendered by their content will need to be managed through support systems, and should not influence interview strategies. It is not usually appropriate to prepare PSRs on sex offenders in the context of 'expedited' or 'fast track' systems of referral because of the need for more extensive preparation, the range of services which may need to be approached, and because the process of moving from denial to acceptance of responsibility and understanding of behaviour is often slow. It is also important to be clear with the defendant about the limits of confidentiality, notably in terms of what he might tell you about his pattern of offending, as outlined in Chapter Three.

Offence Analysis

National Standards describe the primary aim of this section as assisting the court in reaching a judgement about the nature and seriousness of the offence(s). They will wish to place the offence(s) in one of the following bands:

- fines or discharges
- serious enough for a community penalty
- so serious that only custody can be warranted.

Report writers need to be careful not to describe other offences which have not been processed by the Police. If new offences with identifiable victims are disclosed at the PSR stage then it will be necessary to pass this information to the Police. The Court of Appeal (R v Cunnah 1996) has ruled that sentence must be determined on the basis of pleas tendered. If 'fresh and highly relevant material appears in the PSR...' this must be '...canvassed and discussed...':...'so everyone is clear about the basis on which the sentencer would then proceed.' In reviewing the case the *Probation Journal* (1996) suggested that it may be necessary to direct that a separate ('Newton') hearing be held to determine the facts if the sentencer wishes to proceed on the basis of facts in the PSR, and questioned whether evidence from probation officers would be admissible at such hearings given that it would not have been gathered in accordance with the Police and Criminal Evidence Act 1984. This has not been tested to date.

If the PSR is being prepared post-conviction, the court may have indicated its provisional view as to which sentencing band it believes the offences fit. It is open to the report writer to present information which might move the offences into a more or less serious band. If the Court has not given an indication then the report writer will need to exercise judgement. Sexual offences which are nonabusive (notably those where consenting homosexual activity is illegal but equivalent heterosexual activity would not be) may be dealt with by fines and discharges (although we would argue that they should not be offences at all).

In our experience other offences which tend to be dealt with in this band involve teenagers close in age, or offences with some sexual motive but not dealt with under the Sexual Offences Act (e.g. Indecent Exposure, Nuisance Telephone Calls, Possession of Pornography).

In most sex offender cases the Court will be considering a custodial sentence. Appeal Court Guidelines allow Crown Courts to pass community penalties only in limited circumstances. Certainly most cases of rape, incest and persistent indecent assaults will attract prison sentences, and report writers are advised not to expend scarce resources in engaging in extensive enquiries where there is no prospect of a community penalty.

National Standards are clear that it is the Court's role to decide on offence seriousness. However the document gives the following advice. 'Where analysis of the offence exposes information which the court might interpret as mitigating or aggravating features...the report should draw these to its attention, without using the terminology of aggravation or mitigation.'

Appeal Court guidance on what are regarded as aggravating or mitigating factors may vary as courts reflect 'public opinion' or new concerns. Recent publications (Gilyeat 1993, Stone 1993) surveying Appeal Court Judgements indicate the following matters to be important.

Aggravating Factors

- abuse of trust
- age of victim(s)
- violence above and beyond that required to secure the compliance of the victim
- physical injury
- moral corruption (gifts, favours etc.)
- prolonged abuse
- degrading acts (including subjugation, oral sex)
- threats.

Mitigating Factors

- youth of offender
- mental state of offender
- guilty plea
- genuine relationship (n.b. applies **only** to cases of teenagers close in age)
- no force
- no attempt to penetrate
- impulsive single act
- clothing not removed.

Note that *National Standards* particularly require report writers to comment on the impact of the offence(s) on the victim.

It is important for report writers to be clear that the document is presented to assist sentencing on the matters before the Court. The dilemma though is that some information which the report writer may possess will have a bearing on their perception of risk. Remember that sentencers too will have some of this information (e.g. the victim's account of a rape charge which has been 'plea bargained' down to indecent assault) so report writers are not alone in their struggle. If it is clear that an offender has been committing offences for many years, despite this being a single allegation, courts may accept phrases such as 'this appears to be part of a long standing addictive pattern' in the 'risk' section of the report, but not 'this is the last in a long series of unreported offences' in the offence analysis section.

Certainly writers should not speculate about generalities in reports (e.g. 'we know from research that this is unlikely to have been an isolated offence'). Similarly when addressing offences which have been reduced by 'plea bargains', it may be possible to write of an indecent assault 'this appears to have been motivated by a desire for power and some force was used' but not 'the offender is denying rape in order to minimise and justify his behaviour'.

Relevant Information About the Offender

This section is usually approached differently in sex offender cases than in most other cases because some behaviour which in most instances would be deemed 'worthy' may be part of the offender's strategy to groom institutions, communities or families, and issues which may normally evoke sympathy can often be presented collusively.

Examples of the former are numerous but would include a piano teacher who took the family of a subsequent victim to the theatre; a scout master whose troop regarded him as special and indispensable; or a father who was the chair of the local community group. The issue of an abuser's own victimisation is addressed specifically in Chapter Thirteen, but may be relevant to mention in the report for instance if it is seen to be a factor in an offender's persistent low self esteem, or the development of distorted thinking. It may not be relevant if it is presented by the offender solely to try and evoke sympathy from the court.

The relevance of many issues such as alcohol usage, hobbies or 'being good with children' may be different in sex offender cases than some others, as outlined in Part III.

Risk to the Public of Reoffending

National Standards remind writers that there are two strands to this assessment:

- the nature and seriousness of possible further offences
- the likelihood of their occurring.

Writers should have regard to

- possible patterns of offending behaviour
- the offender's capacity or motivation to change
- the availability of programmes or activities which could reduce the risk or impact of further offending.

The issue of risk assessment is addressed in Chapter Fourteen but the key question for report writers will be 'is the risk this man poses manageable in the community?' One dilemma, already addressed, is that assessment of risk is influenced by known previous behaviour even if that has not resulted in convictions.

Part of the developing art of report writers is to be able to allude to these matters in an appropriate manner which is acceptable to the Court. Even where concerns are very high, report writers need to remember that the offender will be sentenced on the basis of his conviction and previous record only, and a long probation order may afford more protection to the public than a short prison sentence, particularly where hostel placements and group attendance afford extensive opportunities for monitoring.

Suitability for Community Sentences

In the cases of sex offenders it is unusual to consider community service because it is not designed to address offending behaviour and may even present opportunities for further abuse. A probation order is the usual option often with extra conditions. The nature of programmes varies throughout the country so it is necessary to be well acquainted with local resources.

Risk management will be only one facet of an offender's suitability. Others will relate to the degree of flexibility the defendant displays in his discussions with the report writer and his willingness to co-operate with a supervision plan. The fact is that if the defendant completely denies he committed or is at all responsible for current offences, he is unlikely to engage in a programme to address his pattern of thoughts, feelings and behaviours relating to the offences. However, complete denial is not an automatic bar to a probation order. It may be that a monitoring role in the context of a child protection plan would be a valid option to present to a court.

Report writers will need to co-ordinate a whole range of opinions from a range of professionals which might include hostel staff, sex offender specialist workers, psychiatrists or psychologists, as relevant to the case.

When presenting the report courts will expect report writers to describe the programme content, length and nature of attendance, whether attendance is required as a formal condition of a probation order and what other services will be encouraged in order to minimise the risk of reoffending. A frequently used condition in the latter context is one requiring residence at a specific place.

Custodial Sentences

If a custodial sentence is a likely option *National Standards* say that the report should identify any adverse effects for the offender and his family, and any other considerations which the court may regard as relevant to the length of sentence. The Court will have a view of sentence length commensurate with offence seriousness and this matter is addressed in the section on offence analysis above. It may be relevant for PSR writers to draw attention to the fact that if a sentence is below two years, the offender is unlikely to be offered a place within the prison Sex Offender Treatment Programme.

Report writers will also be aware that the Criminal Justice Act 1991 Section 2(2)b introduced the power for courts to pass a sentence longer than the term commensurate with the seriousness of the offence, when considering offences of a violent or sexual nature where it is felt that the offender poses a risk of serious harm to the community. The term 'serious harm' is defined as 'death or serious personal injury, whether physical or psychological, occasioned by further such offences'. This poses difficulty for practitioners because whilst public protection concerns should clearly be paramount, they need to guard against the temptation routinely to overstate risk which will have the effect of prolonging a defendant's period in custody without proper cause. We have already noted that those who may present a high risk of reoffending do not necessarily commit the most serious offences. This too will be a factor in the Court's consideration of what it considers to be 'serious harm'. Risk issues are addressed in full in Chapter Fourteen. Whilst report writers will need to bear these matters in mind, the risk that a defendant may receive an extended sentence should not deter them from presenting all relevant issues.

The Home Office (1992) describes the implications for report writers as follows. They must 'verify carefully any information or comments in the report which might lead the Court to conclude that there is a risk to the public of serious harm from the offender. The PSR should present any such evidence impartially.' It notes that 'report writers should consider whether measures other than custody would help to reduce the risk of serious harm.'

Another consideration in the case of a custodial sentence is the use of the Section 44 (CJA 1991) provision to extend supervision after sentence. Where it would appear that such a provision could make a significant contribution to the management of risk in a case, then the use of this provision is clearly appropriate. Again practitioners should take care to conform to local policy guidance.

PRISONER RELEASE CONSIDERATIONS

All prisoners sentenced to more than one year, whether serving fixed terms or life sentences, are subject to Sentence Planning arrangements which provide the essential mechanism for determining their passage through sentence, including considerations about release. An understanding of that process is therefore useful to all who contribute to decisions about the release of prisoners.

The Woolf Report (1990) introduced the concept of Sentence Planning for all prisoners serving more than one year. The Criminal Justice Act 1991 introduced the concept of a sentence of imprisonment being served partly in custody and partly in the community. Each have had a major and interlinked impact on the systems under which prisoners may obtain early release from custody.

The original Sentence Planning procedures, introduced in 1992, were reviewed in 1995. That review found that whilst there was widespread support for the system in principle there was also considerable criticism about how it was working in practice. As a result of the review a revised Sentence Planning system has been devised and implemented from 1st April 1997 following joint Prison and Probation training. One of the major changes within the new system is a heightened emphasis on risk assessment as an integral part of the process.

The sentence planning procedures are intended to lead to an integrated system of sentence management and the Prison Service manual (1997) outlines the aims as follows:

For the Prison and Probation Services

- to provide information to assist prison establishments and probation services to target resources more effectively, in order to ensure that prison regimes and probation service programmes more closely match the identified needs of offenders.

For the Public

- to reduce the risk of re-offending by prisoners by identifying areas of risk and providing action plans aimed at reducing that risk during custody and while under supervision in the community.

For the Prisoner

- to enable prisoners to make constructive use of their time in prison
- to provide strategies for prisoners to avoid further offending and consequent further periods of imprisonment
- to provide a more structured resettlement into the community
- within the content of lawful custody, to minimise the destructive effects of imprisonment.

The system uses a series of pro-formas which are issued by the prison and should be returned according to a pre-set timetable. This is intended to provide a two way flow of information between the prison and the community probation team and will also draw on information from other sources as appropriate.

Assessments in relation to sexual abusers need both to feed into the sentence planning process and to draw upon it when any subsequent reports pertaining to release are being prepared. There are four main areas which need particular attention with risk assessment being at the foundation of each:

(1) Factors relevant to the offender's possible referral to the Sex Offender Treatment Programme (S.O.T.P.) and /or to community based programmes of sex offence work upon release.

(2) The use of any additional licence conditions felt necessary to enhance the protection of the public upon release (be that temporary release during sentence or release on licence post custody).

(3) 'Schedule One' notification in accordance with Instruction to Governors 54/1994.

(4) The views of any relevant victims in the community in accordance with the Victims' Charter.

Sex Offender Treatment Programmes and Community Programmes

The Prison Service's Sex Offender Treatment Programme (SOTP) is now intended to be on offer to all sex offenders serving a long enough period to allow its completion (in practice approximately 12 months, i.e. a two year sentence) providing they meet certain criteria. Candidates must score 80 or more on an IQ test (although courses for those scoring lower than that are, at the time of writing, being piloted) and must be passed medically fit. They must express a willingness to attend and be prepared to sign a contract to that effect, and they must be assessed as having the right motivation for attendance.

Once the above basic criteria are met candidates are assessed in detail using a 'battery' of psychometric tests and questionnaires. In addition to having an influence on the final decision to accept the individual onto the programme or not, these tests are primarily aimed at identifying those criminogenic factors which the subsequent treatment will seek to address. Also applied at this point is a risk classification assessment and the programmes will target candidates in order of priority in respect of risk. Again it is the Sentence Planning procedures which provide the mechanism for those who contribute to it to feed in all information relevant to the SOTP assessment process.

Progress reports may be sent to the community based probation officer whilst the programme is running and although there may be variations in the practice depending on the case, resources and so forth, there is an expectation that the officer will be invited to attend a post treatment case conference. At that meeting there will be a written report and verbal feedback of the individual's progress on the programme along with specific recommendations for future work based on the tutors' subjective assessments. These should be used to inform subsequent assessment of follow up work in the community and will be useful both in respect of child and public protection measures and ongoing treatment needs. It should not be assumed that those who have completed the SOTP (even if seemingly very successfully) are necessarily ready to move directly to community based relapse prevention work. However, feedback from the SOTP, a programme devised, monitored, and overseen by psychologists with practice expertise in sexual abuse work, should be regarded as a most valuable basis for the assessment and planning of further work.

Release Conditions

The Criminal Justice Act 1991 introduced new categories of short term and long term prisoners for the purpose of early release consideration. All short term prisoners serving less than 12 months are subject to automatic unconditional release (A.U.R.) at the half way point of their sentence. Those serving 12 months or more but less than 4 years are subject to automatic conditional release (ACR) at the half way point and are then under supervision until the three quarter point of their sentence.

Long term prisoners serving 4 years or more may be subject to discretionary conditional release (DCR) on the recommendation of the Parole Board. This can be at the half way point of their sentence or at any point between then and the two third point and is subject to supervision. Whether or not such release is granted all such prisoners will be subject to supervision upon release at the two third point until the three quarter point of the sentence.

Section 44 of the Criminal Justice Act provides for an exception to the above rules for early release on supervision for those serving sentences where '...the whole or any part of the sentence was imposed for a sexual offence...' This provision is relevant specifically at the time of sentence imposition and is dealt with in the section on pre-sentence reports.

The *National Standards for the Supervision of Offenders in the Community* provide a list of extra licence conditions which can be imposed by prison governors in ACR cases and by the Parole Board in DCR cases. In providing contributions and reports about early release, officers should recommend the use of some or all of these conditions whenever they are felt to be useful in pursuit of our primary aim of public protection. The standard conditions available are as follows:

While under supervision you must:

(1) attend upon a duly qualified psychiatrist/psychologist/medical practitioner for such care, supervision or treatment as that practitioner recommends (where known, the practitioner should be named, subject to their agreement)

(2) not engage in any work or other organized activity involving a person under the age of..., either on a professional or voluntary basis

(3) reside at (name and address, e.g. hostel) and must not leave to live elsewhere without obtaining the prior approval of your supervising officer

(4) not reside in the same household as any child under...years of age

(5) not seek to approach or communicate with your wife/former wife/daughter/son/children/grandchildren/other persons or any members of their family (persons must be named) without the prior approval of your supervising officer/and (name of the appropriate social services department)

(6) comply with any requirements reasonably imposed by your supervising officer for the purpose of ensuring that you address your alcohol/drug/sexual/gambling/solvent abuse/anger/debt/offending behaviour problems (name of course/centre where appropriate).

Whilst the *National Standards* state recommendations for additional conditions should 'normally be limited to appropriate choices' from this list, this does not preclude consideration of others if they can be shown to be necessary and manageable.[1]

---

1   NB The Crime Sentences Act 1997, not yet in force, will change the provision for the early release of prisoners and subsequent supervisory arrangements.

'Schedule One' Notification

In considering the suitability of the release proposals of any offender con-victed of a 'Schedule One' offence against a child, or young person it is the child protection issues that are paramount. The procedures for ensuring that these issues are addressed are outlined in the *Guidance Notes* to: *Instruction to Prison Governors: Release of Prisoners Convicted of Offences against Children or Young Persons under the Age of 18* and these must be strictly adhered to.

Victims' Issues

Under the provisions of the Victims' Charter all victims of serious sexual and violent crimes have the right to be kept informed of the progress of the sentence and to express a view about the conditions under which the offender may later be released. This procedure is outlined in…but practice currently differs within each probation area. There is for example no specific definition of what constitutes a serious sexual offence and, for example, Northumbria Probation Service has chosen to define that as any offence which results in a sentence of four years or more.

There may however be exceptions to that on a case by case basis within Northumbria and other Probation Areas will have devised their own systems. Practitioners should therefore check what local arrangements are in each case, and ensure that their practice conforms to them.

Life Sentences

There are two types of life sentence. Mandatory life sentences which are automatically imposed for offences of murder and discretionary life sentences which may be imposed for certain other offences, those which concern us particularly here being rape, buggery and sexual intercourse or incest with a girl under 13 years of age. These sentences differ from all other prison sentences in that they are indeterminate with release being subject to (1) the completion of the tariff period **and** (2) an assessment of risk and danger to the public. In the case of mandatory lifers the Home Secretary may also consider 'wider political considerations' and extend the period of custody on those grounds. Recent Home Office Policy dictates that life sentence prisoners, with either a current or previous conviction for a sexual offence, should not be released until they have addressed their sexual offending on one of the prison programmes.

The tariff period is the length of imprisonment deemed necessary to satisfy the requirements of retribution and deterrence. The procedure for determin-ing the length of the tariff differs in respect of mandatory and discretionary sentences, but that detail need not concern us here. (Readers are referred to Stone 1996 for a full consideration of the lifer system.) What we need to address in both cases are those factors relevant to the protection of the public, i.e. risk assessment. As with determinate sentence prisoners, the mechanism for this is provided by the sentence planning procedures which for life sentence prisoners is known as the Life Sentence Plan (LSP).

The first section of the Life Sentence Plan addresses risk assessment and the identification of a plan of work to address the risk factors identified is a key feature of the remainder of the sentence plan.

The philosophy and aims of the Life Sentence Plan are similar to those as described for determinate sentences and it leads to the formation of a series of agreed targets which must be met before the prisoner can progress through the system. It is central to the management of the life sentence as the following extract from the Prison Service manual makes clear:

> 'It is designed to achieve continuity, consistency of approach and proper communication: it is therefore vital that it is used correctly and kept up to date. Parts of the document will be disclosed to the inmate.
>
> It is not intended to replace F75 reports provided for formal reviews by the Parole Board, but the information in it should form the basis of these reports.
>
> The LSP is a continuous record that accompanies the inmate through his sentence recording his personal growth, progress, and how offending behaviour is being tackled.'

All life sentence prisoners, whether mandatory or discretionary, may only be released subject to a Life Licence which contains the following standard conditions:

(1) to place him or herself under the supervision of whichever probation officer is nominated for this purpose

(2) to report to the nominated probation officer on release and keep in touch with that officer in accordance with that officer's instructions

(3) to receive visits from that officer where the licensee is living, if the probation officer so requires

(4) to reside only where approved by the probation officer

(5) to work only where approved by the probation officer

(6) not to travel outside Great Britain without the prior permission of the probation officer.

In addition to the above, however, any other conditions considered appropriate to ensure the continued safety of the public or to assist reintegration into the community may be added, and should be wherever it is felt they would assist with the primary aim of public protection.

'SCHEDULE ONE' OFFENCES

There is something about the term 'Schedule One Offence' that seems to promise precision in terms of definition and procedures but then fails to deliver. Our experience in providing consultation, advice and training is that this is a subject which commonly provokes anxiety and uncertainty in both practitioners and managers. The search for answers only seem to add to the confusion because there is no one single source of information or guidance on this topic.

Much of the anxiety about this area of work may be lifted once it is realised that existence of a 'Schedule One' offence should essentially be regarded as a trigger to prompt the normal child protection procedures adopted by the relevant agencies.

The term 'Schedule One Offence' derives from a list of offences given in the First Schedule of the Children and Young Persons Act 1933. Reference to that Act now however, provides only part of the answer because the list of offences has been amended on several occasions by subsequent legislation.

The guidance notes to *Instruction to Prison Governors 54/94* entitled *Release of Prisoners Convicted of Offences against Children or Young Persons Under the Age of 18* includes a list of relevant offences but this too is incomplete as some offences under Schedule One of the Protection of Children Act 1978 and Sections 1 and 2 of the Child Abduction Act 1984 would need to be added. In practice it is better to avoid confusion inherent in the law and adopt a working definition to cover any offence of cruelty, neglect, violence or sexual abuse of any kind against anyone under the age of 18. All such offences, whether committed recently or in the past, are relevant.

Confusion also exists as to whether police cautions are relevant. Again the legal authority is unclear. However, given that a caution can only be given after admission of guilt, our view is that it should be considered relevant in triggering child protection procedures.

Implications for Practice

There are three areas of practice to which 'Schedule One' considerations apply; child protection procedures, arrangements for the release of prisoners, and employment issues. In our experience, there are two main sources of anxiety or concern for practitioners in relation to each of these areas. The first lies in the apparent unfairness of a definition which applies the same label 'Schedule One Offender' to a 17 year old, convicted of unlawful sexual intercourse with his 15 year old girlfriend within what both believe to be an equal relationship, and a middle aged man convicted of the rape of a girl under the age of eighteen. Whilst on the face of it this seems anomalous the reality is of course that we can and should be responding differently to each of these cases in practice. The second is in relation to the disclosure of information. Difficult decisions need to be made about what to disclose to whom and in what circumstances. There are no easy answers to these difficulties but we should err on the side of caution in pursuit of the primary aim of child protection.

Child Protection Procedures

As we have said earlier, identification of a 'Schedule One' offence should be seen essentially as a trigger which demands action in relation to child protection. The action subsequently taken should be informed by as full an appraisal as possible of the details concerning the relevant offence or offences and an assessment of the individual case. Every response therefore requires judgements to be made. Reference should be made to the relevant agency guidelines and procedures for the framework within which those judgements are made and subsequent action taken.

Arrangements for the Release of Prisoners

The *Instruction 54/94 to Governors* sets out special arrangements for the release of prisoners convicted of 'Schedule One' offences which '…are intended to provide a framework to enable the Prison Service to work more closely with local authority Social Services departments and the Probation Service in seeking to protect children or young persons who may be at risk when a prisoner is released from custody.' The circular provides arrangements for the prison to notify and consult with Social Services and the Probation Service at the start of a period of custody, at various points during custody such as when home leave on temporary release are applied for, and prior to release. These notifications provide the opportunity to ensure that any necessary or desirable child protection measures are taken and again this requires judgements to be made about what those measures should be.

There is facility for the Social Services Department to decide, as a matter of judgement for them, that no child protection issues are involved and in such cases no further action need be taken. The example given in the *Instruction* is of a case of minor physical violence between young persons of a similar age or development.

Employment Issues

At the time of writing proposals are underway for new legislation which should make it a criminal offence for anyone convicted of sexual offences against children to seek employment or offer services which would bring them into regular contact with children. We await the results of those proposals. In the meantime the Rehabilitation of Offenders Act 1974 (Exceptions) Order 1975 (S.1. 1975/1023), exempts certain types of employment from the rehabilitation provisions otherwise provided by that Act. A range of positions involving the provision of services to persons under the age of 18 are covered by this exemption. Any applicant for such posts must, if asked, disclose all previous convictions even if they would otherwise be 'spent' under the Act.

The above provisions are limited however, in that they place the onus on employers to ask and on the applicant to disclose, and only in relation to certain posts.

Of most concern to practitioners however is what action they themselves should take if a 'Schedule One' offender with whom they are working is applying or considering applying for any position whether paid or voluntary which may involve contact with children. Practitioners should act within their own agency procedures and guidelines but again there will be instances where considered judgements must be made. 'Schedule One' offenders should be made aware from the onset of working with them that the worker will take action including disclosure to employers, voluntary organisations, or educational establishments where necessary.

Conclusion

There are no easy answers to working with 'Schedule One' offenders. The existence of a conviction, police caution, or allegation of a 'Schedule One' offence should be regarded as a trigger for action in relation to child protection. All such cases require some judgement to be exercised within agency guidelines and procedures, and workers should consult freely with supervisors and/or managers in taking those decisions.

Sex Offenders Act 1997 – Part 1 (Home Office 1997)

This Act requires anyone convicted of (or cautioned for) certain sexual offences to notify their address and subsequent changes of address to the police. (This has loosely been described as the 'Sex Offenders' Register' although no separate register exists.) Some sexual offences are excluded on the basis that offences may involve parties who are close in age or where behaviour between males is illegal when comparative behaviour between a male and a female would not be. Consequently readers should refer to the Home Office Circular 39/1997 (Home Office 1997) or Scottish Office Circular SWSG 11/1997 (Scottish Office 1997) for details. The circulars also give the lengths of time for which offenders are subject to this requirement, the time being related to sentence length.

The Circulars stress that notification should not be routine and that risk assessment is 'at the heart of the process.' Assessment should be used to guide inter-agency risk management strategies for high risk offenders. This may include the sharing of information with identified professionals if necessary. Disclosure to a member of the general public will 'very much be the exception to the rule'.

Other professionals may be involved in the assessment and management of risk. The Circulars outline the factors to be taken into account in the assessment, which are

- 'the nature and pattern of previous offending
- compliance with previous sentences and Court Orders
- the probability that a further offence will be committed
- the harm such behaviour would cause
- any predatory behaviour which may indicate a likelihood that he will re-offend
- the potential objects of harm (and whether they are children or otherwise especially vulnerable)
- the potential consequences of disclosure to the offender and his family
- the potential consequences of disclosure in the wider context of law and order.'

Police in all areas are negotiating inter-agency protocols to which workers should adhere when considering these issues.

PART III

THE PRACTICALITIES OF ASSESSMENT

CHAPTER FIVE

Assessing the Cycle of Offending

WHY ASSESS?

Sections of Chapter Two describe cycle models of offending and should be referred to alongside this chapter. The assault cycle helps workers and abusers to understand the self reinforcing pattern of thoughts and behaviours which each offender has developed. Whilst the framework is similar, in every case the content will be different. By understanding the cycle it is hoped that clients will learn that abuse is part of a process and does not 'just happen'. Analysis of the cycle will yield helpful qualitative information to aid risk assessment, including the range of 'targets', and grooming behaviours used, the patterns of arousal and distorted thinking, and information as to any inhibitors the abuser has previously deployed. By understanding the abuser's pattern or patterns of abuse, targets for change during the therapeutic phase of work can be identified. In many cases doing the exercise itself will generate cognitive change.

In the longer term the information gained can be shared with partners, survivors and significant others, if appropriate, in order that they have full information to consider in relation to protection. Obviously this is a process which can be quite traumatic for those receiving the information, and it is vital that this is done sensitively and with appropriate support systems in place.

TARGETS FOR ASSESSMENT

The worker will wish to glean as much information as possible for each stage of the cycle. It is important that this is done using the abuser's own words. The worker will aim to assess the following:

(1) whether the client is able to distinguish the thoughts, feelings and behaviours relating to his past offending

(2) whether there are particular sections of the cycle that the client has difficulty describing, and why

(3) whether more than one cycle exists to explain a range of abusive behaviours, and the relationship if any between them

(4) whether the client can understand the relevance of the cycle to treatment/intervention and the potential for relapse

(5) whether the client can give examples of actions he must take or not take at each stage of the cycle to avoid lapse and relapse

(6) whether there have been periods in the past when the cycle has been inhibited, and whether that has been because of efforts by the client, or whether externally imposed

(7) whether the client discloses particular attitudes or values about his offending.

HOW TO ASSESS?

This exercise is typically undertaken towards the end of the assessment period when a considerable amount of information has become available from other sources (see Chapter Three). Consequently the exercise will be as much aimed at giving structure to that information, as eliciting new information or insights. Like much of this work the exercise can be undertaken in a groupwork setting or co-working sessions with the individual abuser, using interview techniques described in Chapter Three. By definition a cycle has no beginning or end, so whilst most abusers choose to start by discussing their abusive behaviour, this may not necessarily be the case. In addition, particularly where single abusive acts or an impulsive pattern is evident, it may be more difficult to move smoothly from one section to another. In these cases the sections may be completed more randomly, rather than proceeding smoothly round the cycle. Alternatively it may be better to examine an 'offence chain'. This is an analysis of the thoughts and behaviours leading up to an abusive incident. The chain addresses similar areas to the cycle framework and serves a similar purpose. Indeed this is the preferred model adopted by the Prison Department's Sex Offender Treatment Programme based on the work of Nelson and Jackson (1989).

The Abuse

Abusers are asked to give a summary of the types and numbers of abusive acts they have committed. Detailed accounts are not necessary at this stage as these will have been undertaken earlier. It may be necessary to come back to this section if other behaviours, not originally identified as abuse, become apparent (e.g. 'french kissing' or 'inappropriate touching' as part of the grooming process).

It is also important to know at what frequency the cycle has been completed. There can be some difficulty in moving forward with this exercise where only single acts are alleged, notably in some cases of rape but also some child abuse cases. In these cases the offence chain framework mentioned earlier may be more helpful. In addition whilst generally rapists would deny that they had committed other rapes if questioned directly, they may acknowledge other relationships when they have 'forced someone to have sex when they didn't really want to.'

Clearly problems may exist if abusers disclose behaviours which have not previously been subject to legal process. It is important to be clear with the abuser at the outset about the workers responsibility if such disclosures occur as discussed in Chapter Three.

Intense Feelings (Reinforcement)

Abusers are asked to outline the range of intense feelings relating to or immediately following the abusive behaviour, which serves to reinforce the behaviour. This range of feelings is described in Chapter Two and includes sexual gratification, emotional closeness, power, a feeling of being in control, excitement, release of anger, revenge (specific or general) or the pleasure of inflicting pain. Abusers may find the subtlety of describing such feelings and combinations of feelings very difficult. In our society generally men are not encouraged to express feelings. Such difficulties will be compounded for abusers who may be being asked to identify very unpleasant feelings (e.g. anger, revenge) with an activity (sex) which is usually regarded as pleasurable. We have often found that sexual abusers are emotionally limited and their responses tend to be restricted to those related to depression or those related to anger.

Abusers often say that their behaviour 'gave them no sexual gratification'. This may be greeted with incredulity by workers when masturbation and other acts related to sex have clearly been part of the behaviour. Such incredulous responses tend to generate defensiveness. In addition they do not always acknowledge the range of feelings which are related to sex. For instance an elderly abuser may not now masturbate regularly to orgasm to fantasies of his granddaughters, but may experience warmth, excitement, and comfort by having them on his knee and feeling their genitals. Similarly, a rapist's feelings when offending may be extreme anger, but it is necessary to explore the link between anger, sexually focused behaviour and sexual arousal.

If an abuser has difficulty describing feelings related to his behaviour it can be helpful to write up the list above as a prompt. However this can cause the abuser to pick up on feelings which do not really reflect his own. It is also worth noting that abusers will tend to prefer describing feelings such as emotional closeness, than those describing overt cruelty (e.g. anger, vengeance, sadism).

Bad Feelings

The feelings after the abuser 'comes down' from the period of intense pleasure are explored. It is important to understand to what extent those feelings relate to selfish concerns, and whether, even during the periods of abuse there were concerns for the victim(s), relatives or significant others. It is important to be able to understand the intensity of these feelings and to entertain the possibility that such bad feelings did not exist, for example with some fixated paedophiles, sadists or psychopathic abusers.

Justifications

Offenders are asked to begin to identify ways in which they justified their behaviour to themselves during the period that they were abusing. Some of these justifications will have become apparent to the workers during earlier stages of the assessment (see Chapter Three) so workers will be working with the client to gauge how much he understands about the role these distortions played in his pattern of abusive behaviour. It is during this phase of the work particularly that the assessment process may in itself generate cognitive change.

For instance in writing under justifications 'I had sex with my daughter because I was not having sex with my wife' a client may instantly recognise the untenability of that position. Alternatively he may rigidly hold to the position and write it up under pressure. Accordingly the worker is not only able to assess the content of the justifications but also how rigidly held are the beliefs and consequently the amenability to later intervention. As mentioned in Chapter Two justifications may range from fairly flimsy excuses to core aspects of a client's personality and belief system. The former are more likely to include the familiar blaming of stress, drink, lack of money, lack of a legitimate sexual outlet (although even some of these can be quite tenaciously held). Justifications which blame the victim (e.g. 'she didn't tell', 'she led me on', 'they took money', 'she'd had sex with other men') vary in intensity in our experience. We have found the most difficult justifications for abusers to understand relate to emotional congruence with children (see Chapter Two) where abusers believe themselves to be at an equal level of maturity to children and vice versa and those which relate to thoughts and feelings about abuse which the client himself suffered (e.g. 'it happened to me and I enjoyed it', 'I was abused so it was inevitable I would abuse'). The justifications of some abusers who have raped adult women often cause difficulty when undertaking this exercise, because they may be supported by societal attitudes.

When assessing justifications the workers will need to strike a balance between guiding the client using information from previous interviews and other sources (e.g. questions and answers given to the police), and putting words into his mouth.

The workers will need to be cautious because a client may acknowledge something in interview when working in the context of the cycle framework but may talk in less guarded moments in a manner which indicates that he has not really understood, or does not believe what he has written up. Liaison with fieldworkers, hostel workers and any other relevant people is particularly important when assessing this area.

Anticipation and Rehearsal

Readers are referred to Chapter Eight for a fuller explanation of which aspects of fantasy and arousal patterns are important. Enquiries should be framed to try and understand how narrow or extensive the range of an individual's fantasies may be, and whether behaviours in the fantasy are similar to those undertaken in the abuse, or whether the fantasy is more extensive or extreme. If the latter is the case then the workers need to try and understand if this differential remains static, or whether during this phase the abuser is 'ratcheting up' the cycle. Another possibility is that the planned abuses are more extensive and extreme than the actual abuse but situational factors have limited the offending. The extent of the anticipation and rehearsal phase may vary. A pervasively angry rapist may dwell in this phase for days until an unfortunate victim becomes available. An opportunistic rapist might move through this phase very quickly. An abuser may short circuit the cycle by masturbating frequently at this phase having not yet completed the targeting and grooming phases, or being inhibited from doing so (e.g. in prison). Such a cycle is illustrated in Figure 5.1.

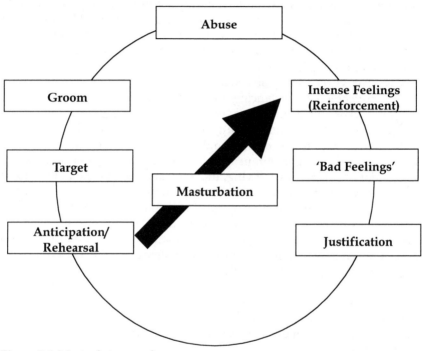

Figure 5.1 Masturbatory cycle

Targeting

Patterns of targeting are described in Chapter Two. Questioning should be framed to elicit the broadest possible response. Targeting relates to behaviour and useful information may be available from many sources. Do depositions disclose the abuser associating with or going near certain groups of children? Were toys, books, videos and so forth found in his house which would attract certain types or age groups of child? Do photographs, videos or books in the abuser's possession indicate interest in children? Does the abuser watch children's television in the hostel? Is there an ulterior motive to the possession of apparently innocuous material (e.g. clothing catalogues)?

Alternatively, particularly with some rapists or impulsive abusers, the individual targeted may be incidental to the pattern.

In addition it is important to elicit from the abuser what it is about the victim which attracts the offender to him or her as opposed to other potential victims. Examples might include a fetishistic attraction to specific characteristics, a feeling of emotional closeness in the company of certain children, or as we have noted perceived vulnerability.

Grooming

Grooming is assessed by exploring how the abuser managed to secure the compliance of the victim and how he secured privacy and secrecy for his behaviour. Victim statements and the statements of partners, carers and significant others are essential tools in guiding questioning. Workers are likely to meet strong resistance because it is at this stage that the deliberateness of the behaviour becomes most apparent. It is also the time when some behaviours which the abuser presents as worthy and laudable are in fact part of the pattern of ingratiating himself with a family or organisation.

The worker will need to be able to discuss the practical aspects of grooming as well as psychological distancing and splitting tactics that the abuser has used. The worker will also want to know how aware the abuser is of factors such as the inherent power in an adult/child relationship which may cause a child to comply with things even though feeling uncomfortable. An assessment of the level of aggression used is important. Extremes of humiliation and degradation alternating with ingratiation and treats may point to sadistic motive. The worker will also want to know whether strategies for securing secrecy involve exploiting an already existing legitimate situation (e.g. where a partner goes out to work early in the morning leaving him in charge of children) or contriving and manipulating situations (e.g. a paedophile who targets a single parent and makes himself indispensable in the household, and gives money to the parent to go out).

Note that it is possible to be misled by thinking that abusers who are not very intelligent are not able to develop sophisticated and deliberate grooming tactics. We have experienced a number of cases where offenders referred as 'having learning difficulties' have acted in an equally calculating manner to any other abuser.

TIPS AND HINTS

(1) Take time over this exercise. It is likely to take several sessions.

(2) Beware the temptation to use leading questions when eliciting the content of the cycle. The necessary skill to acquire is that of asking the right questions to elicit genuine individualised responses.

(3) A useful way to capture the cycle is for it to be written up as the exercise proceeds. Ideally if the client does the writing he then 'owns' the exercise and you cannot later be accused of putting words in his mouth. Occasionally you may need to resolve a struggle about who does the writing, but beware this does not become a distraction, and be sensitive to those whose literacy skills are poor.

(4) Beware that clients do not feel the exercise is an end in itself.

(5) Subsequent information may cause you to amend the cycle. Indeed clients should be encouraged to refine their cycle(s) as work unfolds.

(6) Be flexible. There may be more than one type of behaviour in evidence which may be apparent at different times and for different reasons.

(7) It may be difficult to identify regular patterns with those early in their abusing careers, particularly adolescent, or some types of rapists. It is worth pursuing the exercise but allow for the notion that 'chains of events' may exist, rather than clear repetitive patterns.

(8) A useful tactic to employ when a client passes through the anticipation, target, groom phases rapidly or superficially, is to ask him to imagine going through a film of the events, frame by frame. A minute of film has hundreds of frames and each can be analysed. The cycle calls for detail.

(9) The style may need to be adapted for those with literacy problems and particularly clients with learning difficulties. The worker may need to write up the details and read them out. Some colleagues have found 'cartooning' or sculpting stages of the abuse helpful (Doyle and Gooch 1995).

CHAPTER SIX

Assessing Sexual Knowledge and Attitudes

WHY ASSESS?

Many of those clients referred to us will have experienced significant emotional and informational deprivation during their formative years. This will be for a variety of reasons. Perhaps not surprisingly many of our clients have been the victims of sexual, physical, emotional abuse and/or neglect. The circumstances of those clients' upbringing may well have been chaotic. They may have been exposed to inappropriate models of adult behaviour. They may have missed significant periods of schooling with associated academic failure. They may have lacked experience of healthy relationships or been exposed to distorted examples of intimacy. It is not surprising therefore that many of our clients often lack basic information about sexual matters, and show distorted attitudes towards relationships, sex and sexuality. As workers we should not assume knowledge on the part of our clients.

Before any therapeutic work on offending behaviour can be carried out it is important that the client has the necessary informational and attitudinal building blocks in place to facilitate offence-focused work. For example, it is important that our clients should be aware of the meaning of issues such as consent, responsibility, and choice within relationships.

Our clients should be knowledgeable about matters pertaining to intercourse, conception, contraception, sexual health and the like. Our clients should be informed as to what laws are framed with respect to sexual behaviour, and just as important, why these laws have been framed. It is crucial that our clients have an understanding of gender stereotyping within contemporary societies, and the discrimination and prejudice associated with sexism. Similarly we strive towards encouraging our clients to be aware of the responsibilities inherent within intimate relationships. Broader issues such as attitudes towards masturbation, gender preference, and healthy (non-abusive) sexual lifestyles should be considered. The argument is simple, without such 'information' being in place we believe that offence-focused work will be more difficult to carry out.

The reason for including the assessment of sexual knowledge and attitudes within this text is primarily so that such assessment will eventually lead to targets for teaching, attitude and behavioural change.

A special consideration is that of the relationship between client and workers and the transferences associated with that relationship. The gender of the worker and the client's associated attitudes towards this cannot be ignored. Often difficulties in the worker–client relationship can be traced to attitudinal issues stemming from perception of gender, power, authority, efficiency and the like. Again, to understand such attitudes implies the need to assess them.

TARGETS FOR ASSESSMENT

As indicated in the section above many of the targets for assessment here will be common to those who have any experience of the personal and social education curriculum currently taught in many secondary schools. With respect to the assessment of **basic sexual knowledge** we suggest the client's awareness of the following issues be assessed:

- the difference between male and female bodies and the significance of such differences
- bodily changes and development, with assessment of the differences between the bodies of children, pubescents, adolescents and adults. (Particular attention here might be given to the assessment of the client's understanding of the differences between adult male genitalia, and gathering any concerns the client might have as to his own genitalia and their functioning.)
- emotional changes and development
- the mechanics of masturbation
- the mechanics of sexual intercourse
- conception, pregnancy and birth
- contraception – what constitutes contraception and what does not
- menstruation and the menopause.

With respect to **sexual health** the client's awareness of 'safe' and 'safer' sex practices should be explored, alongside their awareness of sexually transmitted diseases and the action to be taken if a person suspects they may have contracted a sexually transmitted disease. This will mean assessing the client's understanding of what constitutes healthy and normal appearance of the genitalia, and what might constitute a sign or signs of a sexually transmitted infection. Similarly the client's understanding of how to find a Special Clinic should be checked, and indeed their awareness of the different names for such clinics (Department of Genito-urinary Medicine, Special Treatment Centres, Departments of Genital Medicine, etc). Similarly, under the assessment of sexual health, consideration should be given as to the client's awareness of how to maintain genital cleanliness.

Knowledge and experience of **sexual dysfunctions** are areas which will require sensitive exploration. Here the worker should attempt to gather information as to the client's understanding of the nature and form of (1) common male sexual dysfunctions such as premature ejaculation, erectile failure (impotence), ejaculatory failure and pain on intercourse/genital stimulation, (2) common female sexual dysfunctions such as orgasmic failure, arousal failure, vaginismus and pain on intercourse/genital stimulation, (3) the often interactive nature of these, and (4) the client's awareness of actions which could be taken to seek resolution of these difficulties.

The assessment of **drug usage** and other substances/activities to stimulate sexual arousal and awareness of health risks associated with this should this be undertaken.

The assessment of the knowledge of **the law** related to sexual behaviour should pay particular attention to the client's understanding of the ages associated with consent to sexual behaviour (for males and females) as well as a thorough assessment of the client's appreciation of the notion of consent. Some offences will need particular attention, for example whether the client appreciates the nature of the offence of indecent assault, the distinction between offences such as indecent assault and gross indecency, the nature of rape. For clients who seek sex with other men, an assessment of their awareness of what is and what is not sanctioned by the law should be undertaken.

Targets for the assessment of **sexual attitudes** are probably best considered under discrete headings. Some of the most promising tools designed to expose attitudes are the simplest – for example, the 'is it all right to…' questionnaire (see measures section of this chapter).

Concerning **masturbation** it would be helpful to understand the client's level of comfort or discomfort at discussing masturbation as well as the client's beliefs and attitudes about masturbation, for example whether masturbation is viewed as healthy or unhealthy, good or bad, sinful or non-sinful, and the like. The assessment of attitudes is helped by placing them within a developmental context; in other words, attempting to understand how attitudes have been generated and developed across the years.

Many workers believe that **attitudes towards gender** and specifically male client's attitudes towards females are crucial influences upon the development of abusive behaviours, including the maintenance of distorted thinking and distorted values. We support this convention and argue that as with masturbation, attitudes towards women and men should be assessed within a developmental context, looking not only at current attitudes, but also at previously held attitudes and beliefs.

Of immediate relevance here are those attitudes the client holds towards pornography. Theorists have long articulated a link between exposure to pornography and a tendency to rape or aggression (Ellis 1989). We recommend that careful questioning be undertaken in this area. Does the client believe pornography to be harmless? Are there forms of pornography that are viewed as 'a laugh'? Are our censorship laws considered to be strident? Is it worse/better for a man or woman to be featured in pornography? Is pornography associated with offending?

HOW TO ASSESS

One of the most sensitive ways of assessing sexual knowledge is through the face to face **interview**, emphasising the use of simple, open-ended questions, for example 'tell me what you know about...' Crucial here will be the framing of questions in unambiguous ways, avoiding jargon, and being sensitive to the client's vocabulary in responding. Care should be taken to clarify exactly what is meant by the client's reply and particular care should be taken to ensure that the client's use of a word or phrase is understood. Assumptions can be dangerous here. We would recommend that responses are recorded verbatim and that prior to the closure of any interview the record is read to ensure that proper understanding of the client's knowledge is gained.

Some materials have already been published in **questionnaire** form which assist in the assessment of attitudes, for example the Attitude Towards Women Scale (Spence and Helmreich 1972).

In addition to interviews and questionnaires much can be learned about the client's attitudes through observing their **non verbal behaviour**; for example, when talking about matters such as masturbation, same gender preference and the like, what is said and how it is said might be different. Discomfort might be revealed more through body language than through content of replies to questions. Similarly the behaviour the client exhibits towards male as opposed to female workers might reveal underlying attitudes towards men and women.

MEASURES

As indicated in the preceding section, simple measures of attitudes or beliefs can be very revealing. Two examples are given below. The 'Is It All Right To' questionnaire attempts to explore what the client considers to be acceptable or unacceptable behaviour. The Parenting Beliefs Questionnaire asks about attitudes towards parenting and can form a useful springboard into debate as to formative early life experiences.

The 'Is It All Right To' questionnaire

The outline below asks you to think about various behaviours between people. Put a tick in the box if you think it is acceptable for the two people named to do these things.

	Hold hands	Kiss on the cheek	Kiss on the mouth (French Kiss)	Touch private parts over the clothes	Touch private parts under the clothes	Have sex
Strangers						
A man and woman						
Two men						
Two women						
A man and a child						
Two children						
People who have just met						
A man and woman						
Two men						
Two women						
A man and a child						
Two children						
People who know each other very well						
A man and woman						
Two men						
Two women						
A man and a child						
Two children						
People who are in love						
A man and woman						
Two men						
Two women						
A man and a child						
Two children						

Figure 6.1 Is it all right to…?

The Parenting Beliefs Questionnaire

Please consider the following statements, and then rate each according to whether you believe the statements are true or false, or whether you are not sure.

- Mothers have total responsibility for everything that happens to their children
    True   False   Not Sure

- Mothers should always know what to do
    True   False   Not Sure

- Good mothers have happy, healthy children
    True   False   Not sure

- Mothers must not let their children see that they are scared or vulnerable
    True   False   Not sure

- If mothers really love their children they can protect them from anything
    True   False   Not sure

- A child's well-being is proof of a mother's love for him/her
    True   False   Not sure

- Fathers have total responsibility for everything that happens to their children
    True   False   Not sure

- Fathers should always know what to do
    True   False   Not sure

- Good fathers have happy, healthy children
    True   False   Not sure

- Fathers must not let their children see that they are scared or vulnerable
    True   False   Not sure

- If fathers really love their children they can protect them from anything
    True   False   Not sure

- A child's well-being is proof of a father's love for him/her
    True   False   Not sure

- If parents cannot, or do not control their child's life, they are incompetent
    True   False   Not sure

- If mothers are around no harm can come to their children
    True   False   Not sure

Figure 6.2 Parenting beliefs questionnaire

There are several measures designed to assess attitudes towards women, children and sexuality.

Abel and Becker Cognitions Scale

This 29 item questionnaire is reproduced in Salter (1988). Despite its apparent transparent questioning – e.g. 'having sex with a child is a good way for an adult to teach the child about sex', 'It is better to have sex with your child (or someone else's child) than to have an affair' – the scale has been much used to assist in the evaluation of clients referred for community based treatment.

The respondent considers each item and responds on a five point rating scale ranging from 1 (strongly agree) to 5 (strongly disagree). The scale is designed to assess the thoughts, ideas and attitudes men might use to excuse their sexual behaviour with children.

Children and Sex Cognitions Scale (Beckett R.)

This scale used in Beckett *et al.*'s research (Beckett *et al.* 1994) is described as an 86 item questionnaire yielding an 'Emotional Congruence' score and 'Cognitive Distortion' score. Beckett *et al.* (1994) described the scale as unpublished in their report. They refer also to a Cognitive Distortion Sub Scale of a test called the Children and Sex Questionnaire (Beckett, unpublished), describing their sub scale as 'a fifteen item scale designed to assess an individual's belief about children and their sexuality'. The reader is referred to the project report (Beckett *et al.* 1994) for further descriptions of the use of this material.

Attitudes towards Women Scale (Spence J.T. and Helmreich R.L.(1972))

Salter 1988 and Prentky and Edmunds (1997) both reproduce a 15 item version of this test designed to assess 'opinions about the rights and roles of women'. A rating scale (agree strongly, agree mildly, disagree mildly, disagree strongly) is used across the items which include 'it is insulting to women to have the 'obey' clause remain in the marriage service', 'sons in a family should be given more encouragement to go to college than daughters', and 'it is ridiculous for a woman to run a locomotive and for a man to darn socks'.

Grubin and Gunn (1990) present a reduced 13 item 'modified attitudes to women scale' in their monograph on their study of imprisoned rapists and rape.

Hanson Sex Attitude Questionnaire (Hanson R.K. (1994))

Items on this scale are rated on a five point scale ranging from 'completely agree' to 'completely disagree'. The subscales and examples are given below:

- **Sexual Entitlement** (9 items: 'everyone is entitled to sex', 'a person should have sex whenever it is needed').
- **Sexy Children** (11 items: 'some children are mature enough to enjoy sex with adults', 'the innocent look of young girls makes them more attractive').

- **Frustration** (5 items: 'I don't have sex as often as I would like to').
- **Affairs** (3 items: 'a man can have sex outside his marriage and still love his wife').
- **Sex Affection Confusion** (8 items: 'it is impossible to really love someone until you have had sex with them', 'all kissing is a type of sex').
- **Sexual Harm** (10 items: 'as long as a child does not protest, it is okay to touch his or her genitals', 'children can easily forgive parents if they have sex with them').

Prentky and Edmunds (1997) reproduce this questionnaire.

Other Materials

Questionnaires dealing with attitudes towards rape or hostility include the following:

- *Attitudes Towards Rape Questionnaire*
  Field, H. (1978)
- *Bumby Cognitive Distortions Scale*
  Bumby, K.M. (1996)
  (the rape and molest scales are reproduced in Prentky and Edmunds, 1997)
- *Hostility Towards Women Scale*
  Check, J.V.P. (1985) (reproduced in Prentky and Edmunds 1997)
- *Rape Attitude Scale*
  Hall, E.R., Howard, J. A. and Boezio, S.L. (1986)
- *Rape Myth Acceptance Scale*
  (Also known as the Burt Rape Myth Acceptance Scale)
  Burt, M.R. (1980)
  Reproduced in both Salter (1988) and Prentky and Edmunds (1997)
- *Sexual Experiences Survey*
  Koss, M.P. and Gross, C (1982)
- *Rape Stereotype Scale*
  Reproduced in Prentky and Edmunds (1997)
- Rape Supportive Attitude Scale
  Lottes (1988)
  Reproduced in Prentky and Edmunds (1997)
- Reference is also made to work by Nelson (1979) in exploring attitudes about women, in Hall *et al.* (1993)

Finally, as work progresses to explore the links between domestic violence and intimate sexual violence within families, reports can be found of instruments assessing the quality of such violence, for example the *Conflict Tactics Scale*, Strauss (1979).

TIPS AND HINTS

Those professionals from health and social work backgrounds who work to assess and treat sexual abusers often forget to draw upon local expertise when assessing sexual knowledge and attitudes. There are many teachers trained to help children and adolescents develop sexual knowledge and learn healthy sexual attitudes. Many have quite excellent materials which might be drawn upon to assist in the assessment process. It is worth remembering that special materials have been developed for people with learning difficulties which will be familiar to special needs teachers. Some might be willing to be involved in co-assessing clients and advising further on subsequent training and teaching.

The assessment of sexual attitudes is a complex and, often subjective business. To assess properly requires a considerable degree of self awareness and understanding of one's own sexual attitudes and beliefs. It is recommended that before attempting to assess a client the worker should answer any questionnaires or test materials to be used with that client, and also reflect on questions that the client will be asked at interview. If possible the outcome of such self assessment should be shared with a trusted colleague, supervisor or consultant and any issue arising from self assessment be reflected upon and dealt with.

In this area of assessment, as in others, the most valid information will be obtained when the client is at ease, has a rapport with and trust of the assessor, and fully understands the purpose of the assessment task. Therefore, particular efforts should be taken to prepare the client for assessment of sexual knowledge and attitudes and clarify any misunderstandings or misconceptions the client may have about the purpose of the assessment.

Some clients will pretend to have knowledge beyond that possessed, for example so as to impress the assessor and so as not to appear ignorant. Again it will be important to have established proper rapport and contracting with the client, stressing the importance of openness and preparedness to admit ignorance.

Some of those assessing sexual abusers will be dealing with clients who have already been assessed and perhaps even received counselling or treatment from other sources. Sometimes clients present as having learned the language of previous challenges, particularly about sexual attitudes. Clients in this situation can then offer well rehearsed explanations or examples of attitudes they believe they should hold, whilst not really holding them at all. Such clients have learned a verbal response which does not match their emotional one. Assessors should be alert to this possibility and hence should check with each client the nature and substance of any previous work undertaken on sexual attitudes, attempting thereby to separate genuine from disingenuous beliefs.

CHAPTER SEVEN

Assessing Distorted Thinking

WHY ASSESS?

Murphy (1990) describes cognitive distortions as self statements made by abusers which allow them to deny, minimise, justify, or rationalise their behaviour. There are varying opinions expressed as to how causative such thoughts are. Murphy argues that within a cognitive-behavioural model, these 'cognitive' factors are not seen as direct causes of deviant sexual behaviour, but as steps offenders go through to justify their behaviours and which serve to maintain their behaviour. In contrast he suggests that a feminist 'perspective' implies that attitudes supportive of rape have more etiological significance in the causation of sexual aggression.

Bandura (1977) identifies three functions of distorted thinking: it is used to make reprehensible behaviour more acceptable, to misconstrue the consequences of behaviour, and to attribute blame to others. Segal and Stermac (1990) remind us that whilst child abusers often hold views which are clearly contrary to those held by non-abusers in the community, the views of some rapists about their behaviour towards women, whilst used to drive their own behaviour, are not dissimilar to views held by prisoners who have not been convicted of sexual assaults, and indeed many non-rapists in the community.

Distorted thinking appears explicitly as a contributory factor to offending in Finkelhor's (1986) four factor model as one of the commonest ways in which abusers overcome their 'internal inhibitors.' Finkelhor also found that many child abusers have a degree of 'emotional congruence' with children, considering themselves to be equal in relationships with them and deriving emotional satisfaction from contact with them.

Distorted thinking also appears as a factor in the 'Cycle' model described in Chapters Two and Five. In this model it appears explicitly in that part of the cycle describing how abusers overcome their negative feelings by justifying their behaviour. It will also be evident at other stages of the cycle, for instance in terms of their views about harm to victims, their distorted fantasies, or the attribution of sexual intent to very young children during 'grooming'.

If we accept such models it is necessary to know the nature, form and extent of those 'thinking errors' which drive and maintain the abusive behaviours, as they are a key target for change if behaviour is to be controlled long term.

Distorted thinking may also be used as an index of change. By comparing the range and form of various thinking errors at key stages of treatment with those elicited during initial assessment, a measure of a client's progress might be made.

Similarly, a further reason for assessing distorted thinking is that the extent of an abuser's distorted thinking, and the rigidity of those thoughts will give an indication as to the likely difficulty in succeeding with any intervention, and in that sense may well be an indicator of the likelihood of relapse.

One form of distorted thinking which has received particular attention by those who work with sexual abusers is that of denial. Denial here is considered to be a multi-faceted phenomenon which reflects a desire on the part of the perpetrator to avoid acknowledgement of the details and ramifications of offending behaviour. In that sense it shares a substrate with other thinking errors.

Denial is manifest in various ways. Denial of abuse having occurred, denial of having 'perpetrated' abuse, denial of full or part responsibility for commission of abusive acts, denial of harm to victim during abuse, denial of the likelihood of further abuse occurring, and denial of the impact of abuse on significant others are the main issues.

Chaffin (1997) reminds us to be cautious in distinguishing 'denial' (a psychological defence mechanism) from 'lying' (a social behaviour) and from being mistaken or misguided (a human frailty). 'Lying is often motivated by fear of consequences, particularly short term consequences whereas denial might be thought of as motivated by a need to maintain a favourable image of self or important others or by fear of overwhelming aversive emotion'.

As with those general comments above, the assessment of denial is often deemed crucial by practitioners as an index of the 'workability' or treatability of the client. Indeed many programmes, both community based or institutional are reluctant to accept clients into counselling or treatment if outright denial of the commission of abuse or responsibility for abuse is expressed. Some workers would argue that denial is predictive of longer term resistance to treatment. Hence assessment of denial might indicate a notion of likely speed or rate of treatment.

Denial is as Chaffin suggests a phenomenon which can serve to enable the abuser to avoid facing the internal discomfort of awareness of offending. In that sense denial serves to maintain pro-offending thoughts, behaviours and beliefs. A detailed assessment of denial therefore might help in identifying targets for cognitive intervention.

TARGETS FOR ASSESSMENT

The most immediate and accessible area for assessment is descriptive, i.e. the content of the distortions themselves. These may include attempts by abusers to attribute responsibility for their own behaviour to other people, notably the victim but often partners, employers, professionals, or family members. Abusers may tend to blame or excuse their behaviour on circumstances such as financial pressure, bereavement, job loss or other stresses. Often relationship difficulties are cited when in fact the offender has himself generated those difficulties. There is a tendency for abusers to minimise the extent of the abuse or the effects on the victims or attribute characteristics to the victim which are not real.

As in most areas it is necessary to assess distortions at the level of thinking, feeling and behaviour. An offender may think that children enjoy sex with adults, which is reinforced by feelings of emotional closeness to children at an inappropriate level, and behave in a way which he believes is appropriate but which is indeed part of the 'grooming' process.

Cognitive distortions will vary in their rigidity and depth. It is important to know how deeply held the abuser's views are as this will give key information about the likely success of long term intervention.

The history and development of the distortions is important because if we believe that these distortions are a result of learning experiences then the depth of learning will indicate how difficult it will be to develop alternative perceptions. For instance, an incest perpetrator with relatively late onset of his behaviour, who has chosen to blame drink for his offending, because it eases the burden of responsibility, may be able to relinquish that belief relatively easily. Conversely a paedophile who believes boys enjoy being abused because he has had numerous victims who have never displayed discomfort to him and (so far as he knows) have never told anyone, who was multiply abused as a child experiencing arousal and reward systems, and has not experienced consenting sexual relationships between loving adult partners, may find it impossible to shift his perceptions.

The relationship of mood to thoughts is an important target for assessment particularly for some groups of rapists but also for many child abusers. A rapist may be able to give rational thought to a suggestion during interview that women do not really like violence during sex. However, if he is provoked into anger (or wakes up angry) he may well masturbate to relieve that anger to a fantasy about rape, reinforcing his former belief. Malamuth (1981) has illustrated that some men are more prone to sexual aggression when feeling aggrieved at women. Most people have said things they regret or behaved not entirely rationally when in a negative mood. Sexual abusers tend to have more difficulty coping with difficult emotions so this tendency is likely to be exaggerated.

If an abuser has strong urges and cravings to indulge in sexual abuse or masturbation as a precursor to abuse, this may influence how strongly he is able to rationalise his behaviour. It is important to consider therefore the relationship between urges and cravings and cognitions.

It is useful to know how an abuser perceives and manages external circumstances which are potential sources of stimulation. Such situations are common. Does he believe that women can dress how they like, or that if they wear short skirts they are responsible for attacks on themselves? How would he perceive a child who innocently asked him the time? Might he view this as an overture to more intimate contact?

Cognitive distortions may vary depending on the degree of sobriety or intoxication of the abuser, consequently any link with drinking and/or drug taking needs to be explored (see Chapter Twelve).

In the cognitive behavioural model it is generally felt that cognitive distortions are a result of learning experiences and, depending on the depth of learning, may be able to be 'unlearned' or modified. However, it is important to note that some abusers may have personality disorders, learning disabilities or mental health problems which are likely to inhibit the understanding of the role of distortions, and any effort to explore alternative perspectives. If such blocks to reasoning become apparent then it will be necessary to refer for specialist psychiatric or psychological assessment as to the implications for treatability and risk.

HOW TO ASSESS

The interview situation is likely to yield much information about an abuser's thinking. It is important that interviews are structured in a way that facilitates the flow of information. A balance needs to be struck between precise questioning to elicit specific information, and more open questions which many encourage the abuser to talk more freely. When assessing for evidence of distorted thinking it is essential not to challenge statements too early as this will provoke defensiveness with a subsequent closing down of the information or the client simply 'talking the talk'.

To assess the rigidity of perceptions it may be necessary to invite alternative explanations (for example, if an abuser insists that a rape victim did not tell because she did not mind, then explore other possibilities the client may be asked only eventually offering alternatives such as that she may have been frightened). Similarly the client may be asked to compare what he said and did alongside with that said and done by the victim, for example as outlined in his or her statement.

Formal structured interviews can be helpful when exploring the above. An example of this is given in the materials section of this chapter. Such questioning will elicit distortions, not only directly but may begin to yield information about how the abuser has set up situations which he has subsequently used to justify his behaviour (e.g. abusers who complain about the state of the relationship with their partner have often acted to deliberately sabotage that relationship).

Questionnaires are widely used in sex offender assessment. There is some debate in the literature about their usefulness. Beckett (1994) suggests that they are susceptible to faking whilst Salter (1989) believes this is less of a problem. Murphy (1990) expresses caution about their use. As indicated in Chapter Three, our view is that questionnaires should not be relied upon solely, but they are sometimes useful to elicit patterns of thinking and as a basis for discussion.

Inevitably quite subtle phrasing is often used which is difficult for many abusers to follow. Even straightforward questions are sometimes difficult for those of lower intellectual capacity and all questionnaires are a problem for those with literacy problems.

Documentary analysis might also be helpful, for example reading the detail of the client's record of interview with the police at the time of interrogation, reading descriptions given by the perpetrator to those investigating matters early in the history of the case, listening to audio tapes of the client being interviewed by the police and the like. Simple check lists might aid the investigation and recording of thinking errors. The assessment of distorted thinking is in part a subjective process. We are comparing what a client discloses or explains with what we understand to be an 'objective' and 'real' account of events.

It is essential therefore that information is gathered from a range of sources to compare explanations with what the client is saying. This may include statements made by victims, non abusing partners, teachers, family friends, relatives, medical specialists, and so on, such as will be included in the prosecution papers. The contrast between the observations and narratives of such people and those of the client will give a pointer to the nature and extent of distorted thinking.

It is also essential to consult workers and others involved in the case, who may have observed behaviour of the client in more natural settings and where the client may be less self-censoring than in a formal interview.

MEASURES

Beckett *et al.* (1994) refer to methods used in the STEP research which were designed to assess distorted thinking. The Children and Sex Cognition Scale developed by Beckett and described as an (unpublished) 86 item questionnaire which yields a 'cognitive distortion' score and an 'emotional congruence' score. The STEP team refer also to Proctor's (1994) 'Sex Offence Attitudes Questionnaire' which is described as measuring, via four sub scales, 'denial of planning, minimization of victim harm, denial of future risk, and absolute denial'.

Cowburn, Wilson and Loewenstein (1992) describe the use of a distinct technique 'to obtain a graphic representation of the proportion of responsibility the offender accepts for his offending behaviour' – The Blame Cake. In this method the client is offered a circle drawn on a sheet of paper representing 'the total amount of responsibility for his victim being sexually assaulted'. Having made a list of who might be considered responsible the client is asked to represent the amount of their responsibility by drawing different sized segments on the circle.

Bays, Freeman-Longo, and Hilderbran (1990) describe in their 'workbook for clients in treatment' the rationale underpinning the need to control deviant thoughts, and an assignment to help clients record thought patterns to be worked on.

The preceding chapter has referred to materials assessing attitudes to children, women and sexual behaviour, and some overlap here is to be noted with the assessment of distorted thinking.

TIPS AND HINTS

- Be prepared to hear bizarre and offensive views, notably about victims, but also about other groups; e.g. 'children', 'women', and 'homosexuals'. Workers will be made aware of views which abusers use to justify their behaviour, sometimes, as in the case of rape myths, views which are common in many portions of the community. It is important not to challenge these views too prematurely. Before challenge or confrontation occur we need to understand and record the range and extent of distorted thinking. It is easy for our own feelings of discomfort generated by what we hear from our clients to prejudice the objective collection of assessment data.

- Following on from the above it is essential that the worker has support to help with feelings of disgust, frustration and anger. This is for the worker's welfare and so as to maintain objectivity.

- Don't try to change distorted views during the assessment phase. Whilst it is necessary to check the flexibility or otherwise of an abuser's viewpoint, challenges too early may engender defensiveness and a closing down of information.

- Distorted thinking is multi-faceted, so try to elicit as many aspects of distorted thinking as possible.

- Avoid jargon which abusers can use to give the impression of progress.

- It is helpful to record comments verbatim if possible.

CHAPTER EIGHT

Assessing Sexual Arousal and Sexual Fantasy

WHY ASSESS?

Chapter Five outlines the assessment of patterns or 'cycles' of offending. It is hypothesised that one of the essential stages of a cycle is that of the client fantasising about abusing, the abuser's fantasy life supposedly compensating for disturbances in mood states. For the habitual abuser, sexual fantasy is something which is activated at times of stress and strong negative (occasionally positive) emotional states. The abuser retreats into his world of sexual fantasising, rather like an alcoholic might return to drink.

It is suggested that fantasy has the potential to drive the urge to abuse and reinforce the behaviour. The association of images of offending with the arousal of masturbation and ejaculation has been considered to contribute to the maintenance of inappropriate behaviour through simple conditioning processes. The pleasure of masturbation is linked to fantasies of offending.

Fantasy can help the abuser elaborate and refine schemes and strategies for abuse. The abuser can practice the abuse 'in his head' prior to its commission, or re-live past offences, embellishing unfulfilled or unsatisfying moments at will.

Fantasy could possibly drive the escalation of abusing. Anecdotally we know of clients who have not found their initial abusive behaviour satisfying, and who have subsequently rehearsed more intensive, aggressive, or humiliating acts in fantasy prior to committing them in reality.

Sexual arousal, often an accompaniment to fantasising, signals a clear danger signal that progression to abusing is possible if not likely. Freda Briggs' (1995), *From Victim to Offender: How Child Sexual Abuse Victims become Offenders*, contains perpetrators' accounts of their developmental experiences. One such man, 'Little Jim' makes the relevance of sexual arousal to offending clear:

> 'To stop abuse from occurring, there has to be early identification of the risk. I have to spot seductive children before sexual arousal occurs so that I withdraw from situations which might increase temptation. I have to identify the signs of sexual interest at the very early stages and get away. Once arousal has occurred, it becomes more difficult to step back from the situation.' (Briggs 1995)

Sexual arousal in its broadest sense is not just about sexual fantasy. It describes physiological changes, including those unseen and subtle changes in heart rate and blood pressure, as well as observable changes, for example penile changes and pupillary changes. It describes cognitive changes, i.e. the stuff of fantasy and thought. It also describes behavioural change, for example behaviour which might lead to fulfilment of the sexual drive. There have been various technologies developed to help clients control their sexual fantasies and sexual arousal. These are described by Maletzky (1991). A full description of these behavioural techniques (e.g. techniques such as aversive behaviour rehearsal, plethysmographic biofeedback, fading techniques and assisted covert sensitisation) is beyond the scope of the book, and the reader is referred to Maletzky (1991) for details.

The assessment of sexual arousal is dealt with in Maletzky's text by Kevin McGovern (Maletzky 1991). McGovern places emphasis on the implementation of physiological procedures to assist in assessment, arguing the objectivity of penile plethysmographic evaluation in particular. He notes there may well be differences between an individual's verbal estimate of his arousal and that measured. He notes that other physiological assessments of sexual arousal have been abandoned (measures of skin conductance, cardio-vascular changes, and breathing changes) or are still being developed (e.g. pupillary responses).

Less intrusive techniques which can assist in the assessment of sexual arousal (card sort and questionnaire methods) are described in this chapter.

We need to assess arousal therefore to know in what way arousal, including fantasy, contributes to the maintenance or escalation of offending behaviour, and to ascertain whether the client can recognise, disclose, and control both abuse and non-abuse related arousal.

TARGETS FOR ASSESSMENT

There are at least two areas of assessment worthy of attention when evaluating fantasy, first the client's descriptions of the experience, and second the client's behaviour when engaged in the assessment process.

Concerning the experience, it is suggested that the worker evaluate the following:

- the frequency of sexual fantasising
- the content of sexual fantasising
- behaviours accompanying sexual fantasy
- the events which precede sexual fantasising
- the duration of fantasising
- the controllability of fantasies
- the vividness of fantasies
- the senses involved in the mental imagery which accompanies fantasising
- the emotions triggered by such fantasising.

Concerning the 'content' of fantasies, details of those subject(s) or 'participants' within the fantasy should be discerned; for example their gender, ages, appearance, and demeanour. The behaviours involved in the fantasy should be ascertained, including any fetishistic behaviours, as well as the detailed modus operandi of abusive behaviours. The siting of the behaviours within the fantasy should also be gleaned.

With respect to accompanying behaviours, it is important to learn whether fantasising is associated with masturbation (with or without the use of pornography), with sexual intercourse, and/or with mutual masturbation or other sexual activity with a partner or partners, or whether it is the stuff of day dreaming.

Those events which precede arousal might include visible events (such as the sight of a child or potential adult victim), pornography, exposure to other sexual abusers and their accounts of abuse, other 'environmental' stimuli (such as photographs of infants, children or adults in magazines and clothing catalogues, television images, newspaper stories of sexual crime), the materials used in civil and criminal legal proceedings, and the like. Other sensory stimuli might also trigger arousal, for example smells and sounds. Similarly 'internal' events should be considered, primarily mood states and their precipitants, for example anger, depression, anxiety, boredom.

With respect to client's behaviour within the assessment process, and using fantasy as a particular focus here, it is useful to consider the following checklist:

- Has the client been willing to talk about his sexual fantasies?

- Has the client co-operated with recording exercises, for example has he completed masturbatory logs as instructed?

- Has there been any change in the quality/content of the client's fantasies, and if so can triggers be identified for this?

- Is there any pattern to those events which trigger fantasy?

- Has the client reported any ability to control the content of his sexual fantasy life, and if so how has this been achieved?

- Are there influences or circumstances which prevented a reliable assessment of fantasy?

- How can the validity of reports of fantasising be improved?

HOW TO ASSESS

Sexual fantasy is a difficult subject for most people to reveal and discuss. Prior to direct questioning of the client as to the content of his sexual fantasy life it is recommended that some time be spent in education and scene setting. We have found it useful to explain that sexual fantasising is a normal human activity, as is masturbation, lovemaking, and day dreaming.

It is important to describe what is meant by the terms fantasy and fantasising, and to describe individual differences in respect of the activity. Some people, for example, experience very rich mental imagery whilst fantasising. Some people do not experience visual imagery but focus on other senses.

Some people are able to control and manipulate the content of their fantasies at will, others struggle to do so. Some people are able to absorb themselves in the content of their imagery, whilst others can only achieve the status of a mental voyeur.

When discussing the content of sexual fantasies we have encouraged clients to consider their sexual fantasy life as an important aspect of their overall sexuality. It is an outlet as well as a determinant of their sexuality. Many people, perhaps the majority, regularly use more than one sexual fantasy to stimulate themselves. Sometimes several fantasies may be used within a single episode. Sometimes fantasies will re-enact past events and relationships, sometimes fantasies will involve known partners but feature practices and behaviours that have not been indulged in, sometimes the fantasies will be of offending. It is probably more realistic to target the control of fantasies of illegal acts than to promise their eradication.

It is crucial to remind the client of the links between fantasy and the maintenance of offending behaviour, and to use such a reminder as an explicit motivational tool to encourage the client to provide high quality information as to their fantasy life.

Glenn Wilson has written in detail about the subject of sexual fantasy. His early text *The Secrets of Sexual Fantasy* (Wilson 1978) contains a self scoring questionnaire alongside the results of research conducted by Rudie Lang and Wilson at the Institute of Psychiatry. The respondents were asked to indicate how often they fantasised about various themes (e.g. intercourse with an anonymous stranger, hurting a partner, seducing an innocent) at various times (daytime fantasies, during intercourse or masturbation, while asleep) and whether they had performed the act in reality or whether they would like to. The research had organised sexual fantasy into four main types – exploratory, intimate, impersonal and sado-masochistic. Readers are referred to Wilson's original scale in the 1978 text, or the more accessible 'Wilson Sex Fantasy Questionnaire' reproduced in Prentky and Edmunds (1997).

A tool we have developed to examine the content of masturbatory fantasy has been the 'masturbatory pie chart'. The name is drawn from the use of pie charts in simple statistics and graphics to represent the relative distributions of frequencies of events or activities. We ask our clients to reflect on approximately the last one hundred times they have masturbated and to think about the range of different fantasies they have used. They are then asked to display the relative frequency of each fantasy as a segment of the pie chart.

Again the exercise is preceded by discussion of the phenomenon of fantasising, and the fact that many people, offenders and non-offenders, use different fantasies across time. An example of a masturbatory pie chart is given in Figure 8.1.

The value of these 'pies' is not in the accuracy of the segmentation. Indeed, in our experience, it is difficult for clients to recall accurately the content of their fantasies across the previous weeks, even if they were motivated to do so. Rather, the value of these charts is in the opportunity they afford clients to disclose fantasies of offending in a relatively non threatening way. Furthermore, for those clients who are not literate it is a non demanding tool in terms of literacy skills.

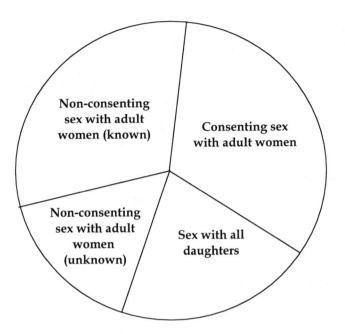

This is the record of a man convicted of incest on two of his daughters. The chart shows that in addition to fantasies of intercourse with adult women, he has disclosed fantasies of sex with his three daughters, in addition to non-consenting sex with adult women, both known and unknown.

Figure 8.1 Example of a masturbatory pie

Once an initial description is obtained of the relative frequency of different fantasies, the client might be encouraged to reflect on whether different trigger events precede the different fantasy types.

   Another simple way of gathering information about sexual fantasies is the use of a masturbatory log, similar in construction to 'drink diaries' used by colleagues working in the addictions field. For this method, as with the masturbatory pie, a contract should be drawn up between the client and worker(s) specifying where the masturbatory records will be kept, as well as how information gathered will be reported on and used to help structure interventions. Clients will need reassurance as to whether their masturbatory practices and fantasies will be viewed as unusual, and what opinion will be formed of them if fantasies of offending are reported. An example of a Masturbatory Log is as follows.

Instructions:

Please keep a record of the number of times you masturbate during the following week. Please record your information on the fantasy record sheets enclosed. As well as recording how often you masturbate it is important to note what fantasies you have used. Please identify a trigger to the fantasy if possible, or record what you were doing prior to masturbation. Record details of who is involved in the fantasy (e.g. boys, girls, men, women) and what happened in the fantasy. The main purpose of the record is to help you. If you are too embarrassed to keep the record then it would be better for you to leave it blank and talk about it at the next session, rather than make something up.

Fantasy Record Sheet

To be completed after each masturbatory episode.

Day:

Date:

Approximate time of masturbation:

What happened prior to masturbation:

What did you do after masturbating?

Description of the fantasy:

Who was involved?

What did you do in the fantasy?

Where were you in the fantasy?

Did you have very clear images in the fantasy?

Did you try to control or change the fantasy?

If so, could you achieve control?

How did you feel during the fantasy?

How did you feel afterwards?

Comments or notes for discussion during the next session.

MEASURES

Sexual Arousability Inventory – Expanded (SA1-E)

Chambless D L and Lifshitz J L (1984). This contains two scales, one assessing sexual arousability and one assessing anxiety to a range of 28 situations, for example 'when you undress a loved one', 'when a loved one touches or kisses your nipples', 'when you hear sounds of pleasure during sex'. Feelings of arousal are rated on a seven point scale ranging from 'adversely affects arousal; unthinkable, repulsive, distracting', to 'always causes sexual arousal; extremely arousing'.

Aggressive Sexual Behaviour Inventory

Mosher D L and Sirkin M (1984). This questionnaire assesses behaviour associated with aggressive sexual arousal (threat and sexual force, angry expression, angry rejection, verbal manipulation, drugs and alcohol). Items are rated on a seven point scale of frequency of the past use of the behaviour. Examples of the items include: 'I have told a woman that her refusal to have sex with me was changing the way I felt about her', 'I have warned a woman that she could get hurt if she resisted me, so she should relax and enjoy it', 'I have threatened to leave or end a relationship if a woman wouldn't have sex with me'.

Attraction to Sexual Aggression Scale

Malamuth N M (1989). This is reported in Prentky and Edmunds (1997) as a scale developed by Neil Malamuth for 'use with college students to assess the components of male sexual aggression amongst those who are prone or predisposed to such behaviour'. Factors described are attractions to 'Conventional Sex, Bondage, Homosexuality, Unconventional Sex and Deviant Sex'. An address for the author is given for copies of the scale: via Communication Studies, University of California Los Angeles, Los Angeles, CA 90024–1538.

The Abel Assessment of Sexual Interest

Abel G (1995). This assessment is described by Abel as offering an objective record of sex offenders' responses to 22 separate targets for sex crimes. The technique is based on the measurement of reaction time to 160 slides of clothed adults, teenagers, young children (8–10 years old) and very young children (2–4 years old). The instrument is designed to assess relative interests in the various stimuli, with Abel claiming the instrument is 'capable of determining deviant preferences even when sex offenders attempt to conceal them'. The results of the assessment are produced in a one page bar graph (with results depicted as scores) alongside a record of self report scores (on a scale of 1–7).

In addition, questionnaires for male and female subjects, adults and adolescents (including a Spanish version for adult males) are available which ask questions of the clients' past history of various behaviours. These are exhibitionism, public masturbation, fetishism, frottage, voyeurism, bestiality, obscene letter writing or obscene phone calls, necrophilia, masochism, coprophilia, child molestation, rape, sadism, transvestism, professional sexual misconduct, contact with prostitutes, sexual affairs, sexual affairs with strangers, phone sex, the obsessive use of pornography, and transsexualism. The client is asked to rate for each of these categories their selected targets, number of victims, number of acts, age of onset, last involvement, fantasies, degree of control over each deviant behaviour, convictions, arrests or accusations, and the extent to which they have received any of 27 categories of treatment commonly used for inappropriate sexual behaviour. The reports from this assessment give scores for cognitive distortion and social desirability, a 'danger registry' and highlight therapeutic issues of moderate and severe concern.

Details of these products can be obtained from Abel Screening Inc., Suite T-30, West Wing, 3280 Howell Mill Road, NW Atlanta, GA 30327 (Fax 404 3510385).

Clarke Sex History Questionnaire

Paitich D *et al.* (1977). A 190 item questionnaire for adults which asks about the frequency of sexual experiences with males and females of different age groups (16 or older, 13–15 years old, and 12 years old or younger) and also paraphilic experiences.

Multiphasic Sex Inventory

Nichols H. Molinder I. (1984). Three hundred items in the 1984 version are organised to form 20 scales, including measure of offence related interests such as child molestation, rape and exhibitionism, as well as paraphilias. In addition, scales assessing matters such as sexual dysfunction difficulties, sexual knowledge and beliefs, sexual history, as well as a number of so called 'validity scales' are to be found.

The MSI was one of the key measures used by the STEP team in their evaluation of seven community based treatment programmes and the inventory is described in some detail within Appendix D of the project report. (Beckett R *et al.* 1994)

Abel and Becker Sexual Interest Card Sort

Abel G G and Becker J V (1985). This is a 75 item tool to be used either as a card sort or questionnaire. Five items are to be found in each of 15 categories (adult homosexual and heterosexual interest, voyeurism, exhibitionism, frottage, male and female paedophilia, male and female incest, rape, sadism and masochism, male and female sexual identity, and transvestism). Subjects are asked to rate each item on a scale ranging from extremely sexually repulsive to extremely sexually arousing.

Examples of items include; 'I'm pinching a 25-year-old woman's breasts with pliers. She's beginning to bleed. She's crying'. 'I'm lying on top of my son. I feel his hot body beneath mine as I kiss his back and feel his skin…' and, 'I would like to have female genitals'. The card sort is reproduced as Appendix N in Anna Salter's text (Salter 1988) *Treating Child Sex Offenders and Victims.*

Imaginal Processes Inventory

Singer J L and Antrobus J S (1972). This test has 28 scales, including scales assessing visual imagery in daydreams, and auditory imagery in day dreams and a 12 item scale called the sexual day dreaming scale. Examples of items include 'whenever I am bored, I day dream about the opposite sex', 'my day dreams tend to arouse me physically', 'my day dreams about love are so vivid, I actually feel as if they are occurring'.

For a critical review of the assessment of mental imagery the reader is referred to Sheikh, 1983.

Multidimensional Assessment of Sex and Aggression

Knight R *et al*. 1994. This is described in Prentky and Edmunds (1997) as assessing 'sexual and aggressive thoughts, fantasies and behaviour... In addition to providing classification profiles for juvenile and adult rapist...are a number of attitudinal scales (e.g. hostility towards women, hypermasculinity, and global or 'undifferentiated' anger), behavioural scales (e.g. psychopathy, episodic dyscontrol), sexualization scales (e.g. compulsivity, pre-occupation, paraphilias, sadism, guilt, inadequacy, and sexual coercion) and vividness of sexual fantasy or imagery.'

TIPS AND HINTS

Sexual fantasy, sexual imagery and sexual arousal are highly idiosyncratic phenomena. It is easy to make judgements about the quality of reports of a client's sexual arousal or fantasies by making unwitting comparison with one's own experience. Avoid making too many assumptions; rather let the assessment of arousal be exploratory in character. Try to explore and exploit individual differences. What is unique about this client's arousal and fantasy life?

If asking the client to record the detail of their experience of arousal or their fantasy life on paper, assume this will be resisted by the client. Similarly assume the longer the period of record keeping, the less likely that records kept will be reliable or valid. Therefore records which are 'coded' might be more 'user friendly' than those calling for written descriptions. Similarly a relatively brief period of record keeping, say over one to two weeks, and repeated at points during assessment and interventions stages, might achieve more than block recording say over a three month period.

The gender of the worker can sometimes be a factor which influences the likelihood or otherwise of the client providing information of this sort. This should be explored directly with the client in the contracting phase of the work.

It is not unknown for the client to ask workers for information about their own arousal and sexual fantasy life. Such questioning should not always be assumed to be provocative on the part of the client. Nevertheless workers should avoid such self disclosure or indeed other aspects of their sexuality for that matter, unless it can be argued that it is clearly in the client's interests for such information to be revealed, and that in doing so the worker will not be rendered vulnerable.

Needless to say good quality supervision is important when managing the work of assessing arousal and fantasy. Similarly external consultancy, for example from an experienced clinical psychologist, is recommended.

Clients should be praised and encouraged for sharing the detail of such personal information. Challenge and support is needed here, not confrontation. Otherwise a verbally compliant, behaviourally non-compliant client might appear!

Most of the questionnaire measures of triggers to arousal and the content of a client's sexual fantasy life are transparent. In other words it is clear what they are measuring, even to naive clients. Proper preparation of the client prior to them completing pencil and paper measures is necessary, and it is always worthwhile asking questions of the client after they have completed such measures (e.g. were there parts of this test that you found difficult to complete? Could you be as honest as you would have liked? How do you think your profile would look if you did the test again in a month's time?)

Finally, it is not unknown for workers to become part of the client's fantasy life. If such a situation is disclosed to the worker, the worker should record the detail of the disclosure and advise the client that the disclosure will be discussed with a professional supervisor. The client should be advised to attempt to control the fantasies, ideally stopping using the fantasy as soon as possible. The client should be advised of the inappropriate nature of any intimate relationship between client and worker. If the fantasy is sadistic and of assault/rape of the worker, the situation should be discussed promptly with a senior colleague and the discussion should focus on the need to ensure worker safety.

CHAPTER NINE

Assessing Victim Empathy

WHY ASSESS?

Increasing victim empathy is believed to 'strengthen internal inhibitions against re-offending, improve the capacity for intimacy in interpersonal relationships, and contribute to maintaining the motivation to change. With empathy the offender can no longer not perceive his victim's pain.' (Hilderbran and Pithers 1989, p.238) Empathy is the ability to perceive others' perspectives and to recognise and respond in a compassionate way to the feelings of others. Empathy flows from emotional awareness, but an individual cannot relate fully to others until she or he recognises their own emotions. They must be able to identify feelings, recognise their feelings, and then relate those feelings to other people. Victim empathy develops when a person who has perpetrated abuse against another person understands the impact of that offence for the victim, the pain he has caused, and is able to express appropriate feelings such as remorse.

Many men who perpetrate sexual abuse are unable to solve non-sexual problems, non-sexually. In addition to the sexual components to their abusive behaviour they abuse as a way of dealing with loneliness, lack of affection or closeness with others, or as an attempt to deal with anger or rejection. Child sex abusers are often emotionally isolated from adults, lacking in self esteem and have no intimate adult relationships. For them children are accepting and compliant and relationships with them are used as a substitute for adult emotional relationships. By assessing their empathic skills or lack of them, interventions can be identified which will teach them how to cope with problems appropriately and ways to develop empathy.

Sexual abusers adopt blocks to thwart or ignore the development of empathy. It is common for abusers to justify their behaviour and to project responsibility for that abuse on other people, including their victims. They show distorted beliefs; for example men who abuse children frequently say, 'children enjoy having sex with adults'; coincidentally they rarely feel remorse for what they have done, and fail to see the harm they have caused. Some men who have perpetrated abuses are able to express empathy in a general sense to others, but because of their distorted belief system do not show or describe empathy for their victim. Others fail to understand the devastating effects of sexual abuse because the effects are, to them, unseen. Because they want to continue to have sexual contact with a child or children, they convince themselves that what they are doing is not harmful. Similarly such mechanisms are to be found when men abuse adults, for example when abusers convince themselves that rape within marriage is not abusive, is not harmful, or something wanted or encouraged by the victim.

It is often difficult for workers to discriminate between various mental events, for example between attitudes, values, beliefs, thoughts, images and self statements. However, such mental events are often called upon to help us understand empathy deficits. Attitudes and beliefs have earned particular attention. One example is attitudes toward rape. Beliefs in rape myths, such as, 'most women want to be raped', 'she was a slut anyhow', alongside the depiction of sexual aggression towards women in the media, plus societal acceptance of violence against women, result in a lowering of sensitivity towards women and the act of rape.

Where there is the possibility of family rehabilitation the offender needs to develop empathy so that he can respond appropriately and sensitively to the abused child and other family members.

Assessing victim empathy therefore is necessary as part of the process of risk assessment and the determination in part of the feasibility of rehabilitation. This will have implications for whether or not an abuser should be imprisoned or placed in a secure hospital or if it is safe for him to remain in the community.

It is also a necessary part of the process of monitoring change. Unless the degree of victim empathy has been assessed prior to any form of intervention it will not be possible to measure any progress.

TARGETS FOR ASSESSMENT

These can be discussed as a series of questions, as follows:

- Can the client describe the short and long term consequences of their behaviour for each of their victims; ie., the emotional and physical consequences of victimisation?

- Can the client describe a range of additional consequences of victimisation for hypothetical/potential victims?

- Does the client demonstrate emotions congruent with descriptions of victims and victimisation?. As abuses and victims are discussed is the behaviour and demeanour of the client appropriate to the material?

- Can the client describe his own emotions and label them?

- Is there evidence that the client can recognise the emotional state of others and label those emotions accurately?

- What evidence is there of rationalisation, blaming, denial or justification being used to inhibit empathy?

- Are there factors from the client's history which indicate or would explain long standing difficulties in empathy and ability to relate to others?

HOW TO ASSESS

There are a number of ways to assess victim empathy. Interviewing the abuser will provide a great deal of information. Before the interview it is necessary to read the victim's statement and all other witness statements or disclosure material. It is important to know who the victim(s) and alleged victims are, their ages, and their relationship to the abuser. Although statements of the abuses perpetrated should provide full details of the allegations, it is necessary to know the degree of violence used, if a weapon was used and whether or not there were sadistic or bizarre aspects to the offences.

Ask the client what has been the impact of the discovery of abuse on his life and that of others. For example, 'How have these events/allegations affected you?' 'How have they affected others in your family?' 'How have they affected those in the victim's family?' 'How have they affected those who have had to deal with the case?' 'What did you think/feel during the abuse?' 'What do you feel now?' 'What do you think your victim felt during the abuse and now?' 'What do you think should happen now?' (Jenkins 1990). Where there are previous abuses ask for the client's description of these also, and his explanation.

If the offender is in a residential project such as a hostel or a hospital, the staff will be able to provide information about his behaviour in the setting, his relationships with staff and other residents. They may also provide information about his contact with family and friends and on his conduct since his arrest. For example one man we worked with charged with offences of Indecent Assault against his 13-year-old daughter, telephoned her from the hostel on Christmas Eve saying how lonely he was and how much he missed his family. Clearly he was concerned only with his feelings.

Interviews with other family members will provide additional information.

MEASURES

Questionnaires can be useful. The following give an example of general empathy scales as well as more specific *victim* empathy scales.

Interpersonal Reactivity Index (Davis 1980)

This consists of 28 items to be answered on a 5 point scale, ranging from 'does not describe me very well' to 'describes me very well'. Examples of items include: 'I often have tender, concerned feelings for people less fortunate than me', 'when I see someone get hurt, I tend to remain calm', or 'before criticising somebody, I try to imagine how I would feel if I was in their place'.

Levinson Victim Empathy Scale

Thirty-seven items, developed for use with sexual abusers, rated on a 7 point scale ('Always' to 'Never'). There are three sub scales: empathic response, interpersonal appreciation and inter personal sensitivity.

Source: Barbara Levinson, Centre for Healthy Sexuality, 2650 Fountainview, Suite 132, Houston, Texas 77057.

The Carick–Adkerson Victim Empathy and Remorse Inventory

Invites interviewers to rate 'the abuser' on a scale none, sometimes, much or very much, across 40 items ('the abuser demonstrates remorse spontaneously', 'the abuser intellectually expresses remorse based on consequences only', 'the abuser tends to victimise or exploit others apart from sexual exploitation'). This inventory is reproduced in Prentky and Edmunds (1997) alongside information about other sources.

Deitz S R *et al.* Rape Empathy Scale

This consists of 20 forced-choice items providing a measure of empathy toward rape victims and rapists.

Other materials of interest to the reader might be.

The Emotional Empathy Scale, Mehrabian and Epstein (1972)

Hogan Empathy Scale (1969)

Clarification Questions

Finally, listed below are examples of questions victims have asked their abuser, either in writing, on video, or in person. Asking a selection of these questions during an assessment interview can assist in providing information about the client's level of empathy.

- Why did you abuse me?
- How can you live with yourself after what you did?
- How did you trick me?
- Do you still love me even though I told?
- Is the treatment helping? How?
- Will you abuse again?
- Do you hate me?
- Why did you interfere in my life?
- How did you keep mum from knowing?
- Why did you set rules and you didn't follow them?
- Didn't you feel guilty about what you did and tell yourself not to do it again?
- Then why did you keep doing it?
- Do you still think of yourself as my father or did you ever?
- How do you think the abuse has affected my life?

- How did you just ignore my crying?
- Did you ever think I was scared?
- Why do I always feel separate from other members of the family – the odd one out, like I didn't fit?
- Why did you seem the better parent than mum?
- How did you think I felt when you were abusing me?
- Why did you wreck the relationship between me and mum?
- What was going through your mind before you abused me?
- What do you need to work on in treatment?
- What do you see in the future for our family?
- How will you know when you're ready for visits?

TIPS AND HINTS

Be Realistic. By perpetrating abuses the individual has often failed to recognise that his behaviour is offensive to others. During the initial interview with the abuser any expression of remorse or concern for others needs to be examined carefully and treated if not with scepticism certainly with cautious reserve. Often at this stage the abuser says what he believes others will want to hear. It is not unusual for men following arrest for example to cry throughout interviews. As well as making it difficult to gain information, often the tears are for the abusers themselves and what they have lost.

Take Time. Reading witness statements can be very distressing. Allow sufficient time between reading the statements and interviewing the abuser for strong feelings such as anger to subside.

Co-Working. Co-working is invaluable in assessment as it provides support and shared perspectives as well as preventing the abuser from hi-jacking the interview for his own purposes.

Style. It is important to acknowledge that the individual may feel ashamed, embarrassed or distressed during the assessment interviews. Although the interviewer must remain in control of the interview, the abuser must always be accorded respect.

Time. Although reports for courts in particular often have to be prepared to deadlines a thorough assessment of victim empathy cannot be undertaken in a short time. One or two interviews may provide a preliminary appraisal of a client's degree of victim awareness, but an in depth assessment of levels of victim empathy is a long term task.

CHAPTER TEN

Assessing Self Esteem

WHY ASSESS?

Self esteem can be defined as the way a person perceives themself, values themself and rates themself in relation to other people. Many abusers grow up in families where they are not nurtured or cared for. Often they are subjected to physical, sexual or emotional abuse and neglect (Wolf 1984). As a result they learn that they are not loveable, and they do not develop the skills necessary to establish relationships, particularly intimate, loving relationships with other people. They see themselves as isolated and this is reinforced by actual isolation from others.

Whilst there is a debate about how or if an abuser's level of self esteem is a predictor of whether they will commit further acts of abuse or not (Gordon 1996) many writers and practitioners have argued that it is a crucial variable. Wolf (1985) argued that periods of low self esteem are associated with abusers feeling unable to cope with difficult situations and their developing inappropriate coping strategies including sexual fantasising. It is argued that a man who has low self esteem has a negative self image. To make himself feel better he may use sexual fantasies which can act as a means of escape, fantasy previously having been experienced as providing relief. In his fantasies he may sexualise the behaviour of others and begin to target potential victims as described in discussion about the Cycle of Offending (see Chapters Two and Five). In Wolf's words 'unloved and uncared for the offender becomes the hero of his own fantasy' (Wolf 1991).

In Pithers' (1994) study of men who rape women (in Beckett *et al.* 1994) it was shown that for as many as 56 per cent of the men low self esteem was a precursor to their offending. Unable to be intimate and loving in relationships, particularly with women they use sexual fantasies as an escape mechanism as described above. Like other violent offenders rapists frequently perceive rejection (either real or imagined) as a threat to their masculinity. They fuse sex and anger which contributes to their propensity to rape.

Beckett *et al.* (1994) regarded self esteem as an important variable with child abusers as well as rapists and included it in a measure in their STEP research. Pithers (in Beckett *et al.* 1994) has noted that very high self esteem can also be dangerous. Some rapists with very high self esteem are noted as having a distorted sense of their own importance. They may abuse power in order to dominate women which reinforces their excessive level of self esteem.

It is argued that varying levels of self esteem influence what are thought to be other important variables relating to the likelihood of recidivism. The links made by Wolf and others with sexual fantasy have been noted above. Pithers (1987) shows that abusers with low self esteem have problems developing victim empathy. Beckett *et al.* (1994) found that some abusers in their study had less victim empathy after treatment than they did before, and indicated that this may be because work on victim empathy had started too early when abusers had low self esteem.

We have seen elsewhere in this book that many abusers do not believe they are responsible for their behaviour and blame external factors. We have extensive experience of cases where low self esteem contributes to this tendency by allowing abusers to adopt a 'poor me' stance. For some clients it is only when their own self esteem has improved that they can begin to accept responsibility for what they have done, recognise that they made choices in order to abuse and begin to make choices not to do so in future. However the causal link between self esteem and such variables as distorted thinking is not entirely clear so there appears to be a need to elaborate upon the theoretical links in order to progress this work.

Again we have noted that low self esteem may relate to a client's own victimisation, which is the subject of Chapter Thirteen.

In the same way that low (or sometimes high) self esteem is noted as a precursor to offending, so it is also regarded by some as a potential precursor to the relapse process (Pithers 1990). Indeed in our own relapse prevention programmes we have found it necessary to emphasise the role of mood states, including self esteem, as a phenomenon which clients need to manage.

In essence it is necessary to assess self esteem because improving self esteem can facilitate and motivate change in the individual (Marshall 1995). Increased self confidence may lead to the development of the perception of the ability to form significant relationships.

TARGETS FOR ASSESSMENT
Influences on Self Esteem

There are a number of factors which influence self esteem and it is important to know what they are. Some of these factors are described below.

Negative experiences in the abuser's childhood or teenage years may still be influencing the way they feel about themselves, so it is necessary to learn about them.

The nature, quality and quantity of a client's relationships may be important as many abusers find it difficult to relate to others. For example a young man with a large extended family was placed with foster-parents as a child because his mother could not care for him and his brother. He is now twenty-two years of age and visits his mother, father, sister and foster-parents regularly. The people who provide him with stability and constancy however are his foster-parents. Although he would dearly love to have a relationship with a young woman, this is not possible for him at present because he neither has the self confidence nor the ability needed to form and maintain such a relationship. Self confidence and social skill have been influenced here by those earlier life experiences of family disengagement and lack of care.

Work and job satisfaction are also important to a person's self esteem. Many people faced with unemployment are surprised at how their levels of confidence and self esteem are undermined. Unemployment is a well recognised stressor, and as such can be a factor in disinhibiting those with the motivation to abuse. We have met a number of men who upon returning to civilian life from the Army found that being unemployed made them feel inadequate. One man said 'I felt I could not provide for my family. My wife had to work long hours and my in-laws, who used to be proud of me, began to disapprove of me.' His self esteem dropped and cuddling his ten-year-old daughter became a source of comfort to him. He then sexualised her behaviour in his own mind and indecently assaulted her.

Financial stress caused by unemployment or jobs which demand long hours for poor wages can affect a person's self esteem. Although the stress of these situations does not cause a person to commit sexual offences, the cumulative effect may be a pervasive lowering of self esteem. One man with whom we worked was a security guard who worked 80 hours per week night shifts for very low pay. His wife, who had a daughter from a previous relationship, had recently given birth to their first child. Although all his wages went into the home, he felt his wife was not satisfied and that she was demanding more. Feelings of rejection and powerlessness were part of his offence cycle.

Ill health, yet another stressor, can also result in feelings of worthlessness and low self esteem. Whilst we know from clinical experience that stress and self esteem are related, at a theoretical level the link between the two needs refining.

An individual's pattern of self esteem may need to be noted as the way we feel about ourselves can vary from day to day or even from morning to evening.

Emotional awareness and empathy seem closely linked to self esteem. Indeed many clients seem to be emotionally 'starved'. They give the impression of flatness and seem unable to recognise and describe their feelings and those of others. As noted this may be a result of earlier life trauma, and it may determine an individual's capacity to relate to others. Another example from our own experience concerns a 20-year-old man who had been horrifically abused as a child. Both he and his sister were sexually abused by his father who committed suicide when the offences were disclosed. He was taken into care because his mother had psychiatric health problems. He never returned home. As a young teenager he sexually abused two boys. After a long programme of work, helped greatly by hostel staff, he has learned how to control his behaviour, although the emotional 'flatness' has never left him. It seems that for some abusers the inability to engage emotionally can never be rectified.

An abuser's own victimisation or traumatic events such as separation may be influences on current levels and patterns of self esteem.

Abusers who have a learning disability may have feelings of low self esteem because of the way they have been labelled and treated (Corbett 1996). This is an issue which may need to be explored in some cases.

Components Related to Self Esteem

Given the theoretical looseness of this area there are several related associated components which we advise assessing in this.

SELF WORTH

Many abusers see themselves as being of little or no value and they have very low self regard. One man we have worked with was so ashamed of his behaviour that he would not go into the town where he lived or even sit in his own front room. Another man said he felt like 'dirt', 'scum', 'not fit to walk the streets'.

LOCUS OF CONTROL

It is not unusual for sex offenders to believe they have no control over life events. They see external forces, other people, or circumstances as being responsible for their behaviour.

SELF EFFICACY

Low self regard and feelings of powerlessness affect a person's self efficacy. Clients frequently feel that whatever they do will have no effect, no consequence, no meaning, and part of the assessment task is to understand their perception of their ability to influence.

Paradoxically a number of abusers who see themselves as powerless are in reality powerful men with the ability to get others particularly children to do what they want. One young man, with low self esteem, committed offences against three young girls over a period of a year. He persuaded the children to take part in games which he devised and then increased the complexity of the games to isolate one girl in particular. This was a young man with a learning disability who felt that what he did in life had little effect on others and no meaning.

HOW TO ASSESS

Interviews

For many professionals one of the most direct ways of assessing self esteem will be during interviews. Areas such as self worth and self regard, significant relationships, and the individual's belief as to who or what is responsible for the offences can all be addressed within interviews.

Interviews will also provide the opportunity to observe body language and demeanour which can be good indicators of mood state.

Observation

Where abusers are in residential settings such as a hostel, hospital, or prison, it is important that observations of staff are noted. They will be able to describe the client's behaviour, demeanour, levels of personal hygiene, presentation and mood states which may all be indicators of self esteem. Similar information may be available from family members, partners or carers if it is appropriate to have contact with them.

Questionnaires and Written Exercises

Questionnaires can be useful such as the Thornton (1994) eight item questionnaire used by Beckett *et al*. (1994),

Some practitioners have developed simple yet effective question sheets focusing on relationships, social skills and so forth. The Nottinghamshire Probation Service Manual, *Targets for Change* (Marshall and Weaver 1991) is one good source of such exercises. Life maps or life lines can be helpful as they move away from focusing solely on the person's behaviour and emphasise the importance of seeing his behaviour in relation to the other parts of his life. For instance one man was asked to record his memory of feelings reflecting a period of years whilst in the Army, reflecting 'highs' and 'lows'. He repeated the exercise focusing on the period following his discharge, thus identifying a pattern to his self esteem.

MEASURES

Culture-Free Self-Esteem Inventories (Second Edition)

Battle. J (1992). hese materials offer assessment forms for adults and children. The author identifies three components of self-esteem for adults, *viz*, general self-esteem (referring to an individual's overall perception of their worth), social self-esteem (the individual's perception of the quality of their relationship with peers), and personal self-esteem (the aspect that refers to individual's most intimate perceptions of self-worth). The adult form of this scale contains 40 items. Additional to subtests reflecting the three components of self-esteem noted above, the scale also has a 'lie sub-test' (8 items reflecting defensiveness).

Examples of items include, 'do you often feel you are no good at all?' 'do most people you know like you?' and 'do you often feel ashamed of yourself?' Items are responded to in a simple 'yes/no' format.

(Materials available from NFER-Nelson, Windsor, Berkshire, SL4 1BU).

Multi-dimensional Self-Esteem Inventory

According to Prentky and Edmunds (1997) this scale consists of two parts, one yielding an overall score for self-esteem as well as one distinguishing between 'truly high' and 'defensively high' self-esteem. The authors' conceptualisation of self-esteem is reflected in the subscales - ie competence, lovability, likeability, personal power, self control, moral self-approval, body appearance and body functioning.

The source quoted is Psychological Assessment Resources, PO Box 998, Odessa, Florida, 33556, authors O'Brien and Epstein.

Rosenberg Self-Esteem Scale

This scale, as described by Prentky and Edmunds (1997) is a measure of global self-esteem though includes eleven subscales, (self-esteem, stability of self, faith in people, sensitivity to criticism, depressive affect, daydreaming, psychosomatic symptoms, interpersonal threat, intensity of discussion, parental interest and relationship with father).

The scale is available through the author: Dr Morris Rosenberg, Department of Sociology, University of Maryland, College Park, MD 20742.

Self Efficacy Ratings

Marlatt (1985). In this technique a list of potential lapse or relapse situations is presented to the client. A seven point scale is then used by the client to rate their expectations of successfully coping with each situation. The client's ratings should enable problematic situations and skills deficits in need of coaching and training to be identified.

TIPS AND HINTS

All work with abusers needs to be done in a way that respects the person. This is particularly important when low self esteem is an issue not least so as not to depress self esteem further. Workers need to develop an understanding of the abuser's potential for any meaningful assessment to take place.

Reading witness statements or written accounts of disclosure interviews prior to interview can be helpful. An indication of the abuser's level of self esteem may be gained from his replies to the questions asked by police, or might be inferred from the descriptions of others.

'Homework' tasks are useful and can save precious interview time. Examples might include the task of drawing a map of high and low self esteem across the life span. Asking an abuser to write up his life history away from the office can be less threatening than doing the same exercise in the office, whilst also acting as a link between one interview and the next. Ensure that tasks are manageable as perceived 'failure' to undertake a task might further lower self esteem.

Drawings and cartoons have been used successfully in many areas of assessment for those who are cognitively less able. These techniques are useful for abusers of any intelligence level as they may illustrate aspects of their self image which are not readily apparent through other techniques.

Finally, our experience is that many abusers, particularly in the early stages of work, find immense difficulty in seeing any good whatsoever in themselves. Some are embarrassed by, or even resistant to, exploring the issue.

CHAPTER ELEVEN

Assessing Relationships and Intimacy

WHY ASSESS?

For many men who commit sexual offences, their inability to develop intimate relationships with legitimate partners is an important feature of their offending. Abusers are characterised by emotional loneliness, aggression and hostility, distrust of others, low self esteem, and lack of empathy for others (Marshall 1989). This is combined with a lack of depth in relationship skills. Men with poor interpersonal skills may tend to use sex with a number of partners or with children as a means of attempting to find intimacy because they cannot develop satisfying adult relationships. Indeed Finkelhor (1986) proposes that 'blocked alternatives' to healthy adult interactions may form part of an abuser's motivation to abuse.

Individuals who are able to develop intimacy are seen to be warm and sincere. They tend to be less aggressive and better able to withstand stress. Their relationships provide a sense of security, emotional comfort, shared experiences, an opportunity to be nurturing plus a sense of self worth (Marshall 95). Intimacy, and our capacity to develop intimate fulfilling relationships, comes initially from our experiences as children. Children who learn that they are not lovable may develop low self esteem and fail to learn the skills necessary to have loving interactions.

Rapists and child sex offenders have been found to be more lonely than those in comparative groups in studies and they score low on self esteem scales (Bumby 1990). They tend to blame others, particularly women, for their lack of intimacy. Marshall (1995) emphasises the need to assess these areas arguing that substantial change can be made by addressing relationships and intimacy deficits.

Assessing relationships and intimacy is important because of the relation with other areas of work. For example, if an abuser has no experience of intimate fulfilling relationships, he is unlikely to be able to express feelings of remorse or concern for others, notably his victims.

The nature and number of an individual's relationships may also give an indication of his arousal pattern. A number of men at the referral stage try to give the impression that all their relationships are with adults. However, it has often become clear that an abuser has been spending a disproportionate amount of time with children (e.g. by making their home a 'magnet' for children) sometimes of a specific age and gender. This may lead a worker to hypothesise that the man has a primary attraction to children. Conversely a man who has generally had adult relationships may not be so 'fixated'. Care needs to be exercised however because we have encountered examples of men who have used adult relationships as a 'cover' for their behaviour, or targeted vulnerable single parents to secure access to their children.

Relationships and intimacy with others are significant in relation to the likelihood of relapse. Abel *et al.* (1988) found the refusal to accept increased communication with adults to be a variable in predicting recidivism (possibly identifying individuals with a high degree of 'emotional congruence' with children). If an individual is unable to develop warm, nurturing relationships with other people, his level of self esteem may be low and the likelihood of him masturbating using deviant sexual fantasies as a way of making himself feel better will be increased. He may then begin to attribute blame for his isolation on to others and remember the powerful exciting feelings of the past when he was sexually abusing. This may represent a significant move towards relapse.

Pithers (1990) found that a crisis in a relationship was the single most common precursor to relapse. Often rapists re-enter their re-offence cycle after believing they have been rejected or treated in an offhand manner by a woman. Unable to resolve conflict they quickly become angry and within an alarmingly short space of time may be at the point of re-offending. At this stage they do not think of the harm they will inflict on their victim, or of a life-sentence in prison, but remember only how good they felt in the past when they dominated and degraded their victim.

Assessing relationships and intimacy skills is also important in terms of proposing appropriate placements and therapeutic intervention and determining the timing of those interventions. If an individual is unable to relate even at a superficial level to others, then to put him in a group could be very threatening and counter-productive. Individual work may be more appropriate with a groupwork programme following later or not at all depending on his response.

The issue of transference in the therapist–worker relationship is very relevant to the area of relationships and intimacy with sex offenders. The therapist or worker may, for example, feel inexplicably dejected or angry during interviews. Those feelings are often generated by the offender and can provide insight into how he relates to other people.

The risk of re-offending is likely to be greater for offenders who do not increase their levels of self confidence and who remain emotionally lonely and isolated (Sinclair 1991). Therefore it is important to re-assess constantly an individual's interpersonal skills so that by the time he has completed the therapy programme he may be better able to make intimate relationships with adults and be less likely to seek out children to meet his emotional and sexual needs.

TARGETS FOR ASSESSMENT

It is necessary to make in depth assessments of the quality of a client's relationships. A high proportion may appear to be in stable adult relationships and be relatively socially skilled when the reality is that they are isolated and lack intimacy.

Because childhood experiences significantly shape and influence an individual's ability to relate to others, it is necessary to gain information about their life. As many offenders have themselves been victims of physical, sexual and emotional abuse this assessment needs to be done sensitively.

It is important to know how individuals perceive who and what has been good or bad in their lives as this affects how they currently relate to others. Some clients, who have been subjected to horrific abuse as children, often by their parents, talk of their experiences in a very flat, lifeless way, yet do not appear angry at their parents. Marshall (1989) describes some sexually abused children as 'insecure, desperately seeking intimacy who see sexual abuse as a possible model for their pursuit of intimacy later in life'.

For the purposes of assessment it is necessary to know about the present, intimate relationships of an individual. Some abusers initially appear fairly skilled socially with a number and range of relationships. An example was a man in his early forties who had indecently assaulted his 12-year-old daughter. An articulate man, he had served in the Army for 17 years and travelled widely. Whilst on the surface his relationships and social skills seemed good, during the course of the initial assessment it became clear that he was socially isolated, his self esteem was very low and he was emotionally lonely. It is important to discover what are the blocks in relationships with such men. He felt that his relationship with his wife, which he described as good whilst they were in the Army, had deteriorated since his discharge and that instead of talking to his wife about the way he felt, he bottled his feelings up.

For younger abusers and for those who have learning disabilities the blockages may be linked to their developmental stage, particularly with adolescents, or to their level of ability or both. These areas need to be assessed.

It is necessary to know what clients understand by intimacy and relationships. Some have a very poor understanding and will need help to give information about relationships in their lives.

Part of the assessment process is to learn how the client actually feels about the targets the workers consider important. For example, for an individual to be able to develop intimacy with others it is necessary for them to: increase their self esteem, gain in confidence, improve their social skills, improve their ability to communicate, learn how to deal with conflict and discover the benefits of establishing equal, satisfying relationships. A daunting task!

When assessing relationship and intimacy issues, it is vital to look for signs of distorted intimacy. Many men abuse children to satisfy their emotional needs (Finkelhor 1984). Children come to have a special meaning for them and they see themselves as being on the same level as the child. Comments such as 'You do not understand', 'I have a special rapport with children', and 'I love children', are common. One man who indecently assaulted a six-year-old girl said 'We broke friends', implying that he and the child had fallen out; he saw himself as a playmate of the child. Some men spend hour after hour, day after day with children, playing games with them, taking them swimming, on trips to fast food restaurants, or to numerous other places which children find attractive.

Another sign of distorted intimacy is when abusers target young teenage girls and seduce them into believing they are having a love affair. Their self-perception is that they are young, attractive and understanding. They see themselves as 'Peter-Pan figures' and often frequent places where teenagers congregate such as dance clubs.

How clients communicate needs assessing. Rapists are poor communicators as they misconstrue both verbal and non-verbal messages from women. Child sex abusers distort typical childish behaviour as indicators of affection, love and sexual attraction. For example a ten-year-old girl gave her uncle a kiss and a cuddle after he had bought her some sweets. He interpreted this as 'she finds me sexually attractive' and began to sexualise other aspects of the child's behaviour. One 40-year-old man said that he knew an eight-year-old boy wanted him to touch him sexually because he sat next to him on the settee and put his hand on the man's knee. Totally innocent behaviour on the child's part was thus used by the abuser to justify indecent assaults with the help of his distorted thinking process.

HOW TO ASSESS?

As in other areas interviews will yield a wealth of information,. Observing how the client relates to the co-workers can be telling. Some abusers are very aggressive to female workers while others are the opposite, more comfortable talking to the female worker or therapist. Non-verbal cues such as levels of embarrassment related to the gender of the worker, or body posture are important and may give clues as to the clients' ability to relate elsewhere.

Observation

Where an abuser is in a hostel or other residential setting staff there will gain a great deal of information about his ability to relate to others. They will see him over long periods of time and will be able to observe his relationships with other residents, with staff members, and which relationships he may be sustaining (appropriately or inappropriately) outside the hostel.

Contact with partners and other family members, including home visits, may yield important information if such contact is appropriate. They may give a totally different perspective about the nature of a relationship. Contact with carers is particularly important in the case of younger abusers and those who have learning disabilities.

Where there is the opportunity for assessment to take place in a group, role-play can be particularly informative. For example asking a client to role play a situation with his wife will quickly give those assessing insight into that relationship.

Information about the person's lifestyle can be invaluable. A 45-year-old man convicted of indecent assault on boys between the ages of eight and twelve years, lives with his elderly mother who is virtually bed-ridden. His routine was that on Fridays he would go to the bank and get out a lot of small change.

On Friday evenings and Saturday mornings he would get out his collection of photographs of young boys and masturbate, fantasising about what he planned to do to other boys. He would then drive around an estate in the city, find a group of boys and invite them to go with him to the coast. There he would take them to amusement arcades, give them the money he had changed the previous day and while they played on machines, he would single one boy out, separate him from the rest of the group and sexually abuse him. On Sundays he would attend church. On Mondays he would drive around the city in his jeep looking for groups of children to target. He had no adult friends. Knowing his life-style led to discussions about his perception of these boys and his distorted sense of intimacy.

If clients have been in care or residential settings, records may yield important information.

Homework

Homework tasks such as writing out life histories, 'lifelines' or network charts can be helpful. Again readers are referred to the Nottinghamshire Probation Service pack *Targets for Change* (Marshall and Weaver 1991) for a source of written exercises.

MEASURES

Of particular interest here is a questionnaire described by Prentky and Edmunds, The Relationship Questionnaire of Bartholomew and Horowitz (1991). The questionnaire is based on four attachment patterns, described by the authors as secure, dismissing, preoccupied and fearful. Readers are referred to Prentky and Edmunds for examples of these attachment styles and to the 1991 source paper for a more detailed exposition of the tool.

TIPS AND HINTS

As with all work with abusers, getting good quality information takes time. Judgements should not be made on superficial information. Often clients are nervous and embarrassed and present a one-sided facet of themselves. At one extreme some clients who have a learning disability can appear far more able than they are because their verbal skills are higher than their reasoning skills. At the other, many who have developed communication skills in 'professional' jobs appear to have satisfying fulfilling relationships whereas in reality they may be lonely and isolated from others and their over-confidence may be bravado.

This is an area where it is very easy to make assumptions from our own experiences. It is common for us as workers to make value-laden judgements about abusers' experiences of intimacy.

Workers must be careful not to imply (however unwittingly) that same sex relationships are less satisfying or valid than heterosexual relationships.

It is important to remember that forging intimate, loving relationships is difficult for a large part of the non-offending population.

It may help to review our own history of relationships and intimacy. Check out with colleagues and friends their experiences and expectations.

There is an assumption that sex equals intimacy. Sexual relations between males and females have many differences. For many men physical gratification is the primary objective because they are more body orientated, whilst for the majority of women love is more important. Marshall (1995) argued that these differences tend to reduce by the age of 40.

There is a notion that 'more is better than less'. Some men boast of the number of their sexual relationships. It is easy to accept that they do not have problems forming relationships, when the reality is that frequently they are afraid of commitment, or cannot move beyond superficial engagement.

Be prepared to be 'tested out'. Many of the men with whom we work have had no experience of consistent relationships. As children they were not cared for or loved. Often they will test us out in the way small children test out their parents. Clients may also ask personal questions about the worker's own relationships.

There may be cultural differences to consider. What could appear to be superficial relationships within families may be the worker not understanding the significance of extended family relations.

Look after yourself. These areas of work can evoke strong feelings in workers, often feelings of sadness and compassion. Whilst it is important to acknowledge the difficulties in some people's lives workers should not shift towards collusion or allowing the client to believe that it mitigates the degree of responsibility they have for their own behaviour.

CHAPTER TWELVE

Assessing Alcohol and Other Drug Use

WHY ASSESS?

Finkelhor (1986) found that many sexual abusers used alcohol and drugs to overcome internal inhibitors in relation to abuse. Our experience is that whilst this is sometimes the case with child sex abusers it is a much more extensive feature of work with rapists. With child sex abusers, alcohol may be used as part of the process of grooming children. Giving children alcohol may trap them into behaviour about which they will be reluctant to tell responsible adults, and may disinhibit the children as well as the offender. In addition, some abusers have been known to target public houses where vulnerable adults might drink, in order to begin the process of securing access to their children.

We have noted elsewhere that the level of an abuser's distorted thinking and the ability to control fantasies may be related to mood states. These in turn are often related to substance misuse, particularly given that many abusers have difficulty coping with emotions. Indeed substance misuse may almost be an indicator of mood state. This is a particularly critical issue with some rapists where precursors to relapse include negative (or sometimes positive) mood states, exacerbated by drink. In these cases the relapse process can be very rapid.

The nature of an abuser's drink or drug use may give strong indicators about their general lifestyle. It may relate to a disinhibited lifestyle which can be an indicator of the likelihood of reoffending as well as attendance at programmes. We have noted how self esteem is an issue which sexual abusers may need to address, because during periods of low self esteem they are more likely to revert to pro-offending thinking and fantasies. Drink and drugs are often used to mask problems of self esteem and other emotional problems.

A related matter is that of 'locus of control'. Sexual abusers frequently blame external factors for their offending (Beckett *et al.* 1994). This is important in terms of how they view their level of responsibility for their own behaviour. Problematic use of drink or drugs is likely to exacerbate feelings that one's life is out of control.

At a basic level it is important to assess the level of drink and drug intake to ensure that an abuser is able to concentrate on the work in hand including attendance at appointments or groups and homework tasks.

TARGETS FOR ASSESSMENT

Assessment targets will clearly reflect those assessments which would be undertaken by specialists in the drugs and alcohol field. However, the purpose of assessment of drug and alcohol use where the focus is on sexual abuse is to identify:

(1) How their use relates to the overall pattern of abusive behaviour, either as a disinhibitor or part of the grooming process.

(2) Whether continued use will adversely affect attendance at programmes and related tasks.

(3) How continued use might relate to the risk posed by the abuser and the danger of relapse.

Consequently there may be people whose drink or drug use would not be given a high priority by drugs and alcohol specialist projects, but whose use would constitute a problem in relation to work with sexual abusers. There are large sections of the British population where social drinking on a regular basis, or regular social use of cannabis is common. Despite the latter being illegal, most specialist workers would not be inclined to regard these behaviours as unduly problematic. However, if after such use a person's judgement is affected to the extent that they are able to give themselves permission to sexually abuse, then the behaviour would be regarded as a problem in the context of assessment.

An additional target for assessment, but a vital one, will be to decide whether drug or alcohol use is such that the abuser needs to be referred to a specialist facility catering specifically for that problem, and if the problem is such that it needs to be controlled before work focusing on the abuse can begin. Some programmes do not accept abusers with current dependency or misuse problems. It is likely that some related work may need to be done if it is apparent that substance abuse is linked to issues which may be offence related (e.g. self esteem, victimisation, anger control).

Bearing these differences in mind it is still helpful to be guided by material prepared by specialists in the field. We have referred to the Dependency Manual published by the Northumbria Probation Service (Gardiner and Talbot 1990) which offers basic guidance. It offers a model of dependency as a behavioural/social problem but is clear that referral should be made to medical practitioners when usage is at a level which is affecting health, or when withdrawal programmes are being planned. The manual supports a policy that illegal drug use can be discussed with clients in order to help them reduce harmful behaviour, but that any evidence of supplying drugs or other related criminal activity (e.g. dishonesty to maintain the habit) will necessitate a referral to the police.

In the initial stages the key questions to address are:

(1) What is the extent and nature of substance misuse?

(2) Is the user able to control the behaviour?

(3) Is help needed from specialist sources?

In assessing these questions account will need to be taken of the following factors:

(1) The history of dependency and misuse.

(2) What substances are being misused.

(3) What cultural factors influence the behaviour?

(4) Present social environment and relationships.

(5) Family relationships.

(6) The medical and psychiatric history.

(7) The work history and financial management.

(8) Potential sources of satisfaction and frustration.

(9) The client's aims and aspirations for the future.

(10) The client's special vulnerabilities (situational and mood states).

(11) The relationship between drinking and deviant behaviour.

Some of the factors above will be affected by the circumstances in which an abuser is placed following disclosure of his abuse, (e.g. a hostel away from friends and family) and consequent feelings of rejection, loneliness or loss.

HOW TO ASSESS

It is important that a multi-faceted approach to drug and alcohol assessment is undertaken. Notably residential staff will be able to observe behaviour at times when other workers are not on duty. They will be able to observe if drinking occurs at certain times or when a resident is drunk, whether they go straight to bed, or make a nuisance of themselves. They may be able to note if drinking precedes or is preceded by mood states such as anger, moping or self pity, or if it precedes or is preceded by certain behaviour (e.g. telephone contact with wife or children).

It may be necessary to refer to specialist programmes or for medical attention in circumstances outlined above. However it will usually be a generalist worker (e.g. probation officer, social worker, community psychiatric nurse) who makes the initial contact. In this situation Gardiner and Talbot stress the need for a motivational approach to interviewing (see Chapter Three of this volume). They publish assessment questionnaires which relate to drinking. Some of the questions would be relevant to other drug users.

MATERIALS

Gardiner and Talbot (1990) present a 14 item questionnaire asking the reasons why individuals drink. These include positive feelings (it is 'refreshing' or 'makes me feel good'), social reasons, or to cope with negative feelings such as lack of confidence, anger and so on.

Mayfield, McLeon and Hall (1974) have a 4 item questionnaire, now in common usage, asking whether a client has felt they should cut down on their drinking, if others have been annoyed by their drinking, if they have felt bad or guilty about their drinking or if they use drink to steady nerves or to remove a hangover. They argue that two or more of these factors indicate an alcohol problem.

Finally, Pokomy, Miller and Kaplan (1972) have developed materials. Their 10 item scale is in common usage. This relates to whether the client or friends regard the client's drinking as normal, whether the client has sought help for drinking (e.g. at Alcoholics Anonymous, from hospital or other professionals), whether it has affected the client's obligations (e.g. in relationships or at work) and if it has affected health (e.g. caused delirium tremens or hallucinations) or behaviour (notably leading to arrests).

TIPS AND HINTS

Be prepared to refer to specialists in alcohol or other drug dependency work if necessary.

Remember to focus on the relationship between substance usage and abusive behaviour, risk issues, potential for relapse and engagement in work related to the abuse.

CHAPTER THIRTEEN

Assessing an Abuser's own Victimisation

WHY ASSESS?

The issue of abuser's own victimisation is an area to be approached with caution. Reviews of studies generally find that sexual abuse is more prevalent in the history of sexual offenders than in the general population. However not all studies of sexual offenders find a majority to have been sexually abused. From the literature Salter (1988) notes that 'It may well be that the majority of males molested as children do not become abusers. Therefore, the paedophiliac orientation, while well documented has never been explained etiologically.'

Ryan (1989) and Rasmussen, Burton and Christopherson (1992) have discussed the possible developmental links between victimisation and abuse. Facets of these include learned behaviour and the abusers' recreation of their own victimisation; traumatic sexualisation; compensation for a sense of powerlessness and lack of control; the tendency of male victims to take out their problems on others; generation of retaliatory fantasies; and identification with the aggressor. Rasmussen argues that the development of abusive behaviours (rather than coping or self damaging behaviours) is more likely where prior traumatisation, social inadequacy, lack of intimacy, impulsiveness or lack of accountability have been evident.

All of these developmental features will have implications for intervention with abusers, so need to be identified and assessed.

By the time workers come to assess adult repeat abusers the time between past abuse, probably many years ago, and an abuser's current pattern of cognitions, behaviours and emotions may be somewhat obscured. However, important links frequently exist which may need to be unearthed if intervention is to proceed satisfactorily in the long term.

Cognitions related to the abuse may be wide ranging (for a more detailed account of cognitive distortions see Chapter Seven). The abuser may have latched on to a fairly unsophisticated belief that because he was abused as a boy it is inevitable that he would become an abuser, consequently absolving him of blame for his behaviour. Other more subtle and deep seated examples include abusers who believe they were responsible for what happened to them when they were younger, so their victim is responsible for what happened to him or her. Similarly a range of cognitive distortions may develop whereby the abuser's recollection of his own abuse primarily relates to arousal, rewards or emotional attachment, and where painful and confused memories have been suppressed. This is the '...it did me no harm, in fact I liked it, so why shouldn't this lad like it...?' group of distortions. They can be further complicated by a lack of perception of power imbalances in their own abusive relationships, which again many transfer to their own behaviour towards their victim resulting in a high degree of emotional congruence.

The emotional implications of an abuser's own victimisation may have a serious inhibitory impact on intervention. Negative mood states including anxiety, depression and post traumatic stress disorder are well documented long term effects of sexual abuse (Hollin and Howells 1991). It is in such emotional states that abusers may resort to the comfort of their fantasies relating to sexual abuse. Many abusers adopt a 'coping' mechanism which involves revenge and the abuse of power to compensate for their own stripping of power as a child. In its extreme form this behaviour can manifest itself in anger or even sadistic behaviour. When such mechanisms are adopted it is likely that the original source of these feelings is suppressed. This has implications for the abuser's ability to develop empathy for others. Indeed in many cases it is not possible for them to develop real empathy for others, notably their victims, unless they have been able to get in touch with their own painful feelings.

Occasionally practitioners will meet abusers where the emotional damage inflicted upon them would appear to be virtually irreparable. This may be an indicator that intervention is likely to be extremely difficult.

TARGETS FOR ASSESSMENT

The primary aim of working with abusers is to minimise the risk of future offending. Consequently the key areas for assessment of an abuser's own victimisation are the effects on cognitions and emotions and their possible implications for future intervention.

It will however be necessary to know what occurred. What type of abuse was it? Who committed it? What was the detail of the relationship between the subject of the assessment and his abuser at the time of his abuse (age, gender, power balance, position of trust, relative, financial position, etc.)? How long did it go on? How often did it happen? Was physical violence used? Were there signs of sadistic behaviour?

From these discussions it will be possible to glean important information. Notably is the abuser clear what abuse is? Does the subject recognise what aspects of the behaviour were abusive? Does he construe grooming tactics by 'his' abuser (e.g. giving money) as him securing some power in the relationship? Is he clear about the power relationships discussed above? Does the abuser believe his abuse has any bearing on his current behaviour. If so, does he try to use it as a justification for his behaviour?

The discussion will also enable the worker to identify aspects of the abuser's emotional response to his own abuse as discussed earlier.

HOW TO ASSESS

It is important that the issue of an abuser's own victimisation is not approached in such a way as to imply collusion with his own abusive behaviour. Thus it is better not to ask too much detail too early. A judgement may need to be made about whether the emotional damage to an offender is such that treatment in the community may not be feasible. However the 'symptoms' of such damage are likely to be indicated during other parts of the assessment process, notably when discussing victim empathy.

The interview will be the primary area for gathering information; this can be assisted by the use of questionnaires.

Past records may contain signs of abuse being suffered particularly if there have been signs of acting out behaviours (e.g. school refusal, running away from home, aggression whether sexual or otherwise) or symptomatic anxiety related behaviour (e.g. enuresis, encopresis, phobias).

Lifeline exercises are an extremely useful tool for eliciting information about an abuser's past. However, because they are deceptively easy it is possible for clients to reveal too much information too rapidly.

Frequently the phenomenon of transference is apparent in interviews and emotions, notably anger, can be directed at workers for apparently irrational reasons. This too can be an indicator of suppressed memories of abuse.

TIPS AND HINTS

The timing of discussions about an abuser's own abuse is important. In some cases it will be an issue which needs to be dealt with before offence focused work can proceed. It is often helpful to acknowledge the issue early on, but it is usually more appropriate to engage in more thorough assessment later.

We have frequently found that abusers want to suppress discussion of their own victimisation.

The abuser will be recounting painful events which probably happened many years ago and where the memory will have been clouded by events which will have had a significant impact on emotions and cognitions. Consequently it is likely that early accounts will be patchy and inconsistent.

The style of questioning is extremely important. Whilst workers should be careful to avoid any implication that an abuser's own victimisation in any way justifies his behaviour, an over-challenging style is entirely inappropriate. However, at the other extreme, workers should avoid slipping into 'rescue mode'.

At some stage of the assessment it may become apparent that it is not possible to disentangle the conflicting demands of addressing offending and victimisation. Consequently it is likely to be more appropriate to pass on this aspect of the work to other workers, whether this be another individual within the same agency or specialists outside.

Part of the discussion may relate to whether the abuser has reported his own abuser to the police, and whether it may be appropriate to do that albeit at this late stage. The abuser will need to balance the likely benefits in terms of possibly protecting others or feelings of relief, against the likely feelings should a prosecution fail.

Confidentiality is not offered to abusers in terms of their own behaviour, but generally it would not be necessary to divulge information about their own experience of victimisation. However, it is important to bear in mind that the client's abuser may still have access to children. He may be visiting the family where children still reside or he may even be still living there. He may be working at the same school or children's home. In such a case confidentiality will need to be breached which may cause serious tensions in a worker's relationship with the client. It is important though that child protection concerns are regarded as paramount.

Take care of yourself. It is likely that the more dreadful the abuse that 'your' client has committed, particularly if sadism or anger are strong features, the more dreadful was the abuse which happened to them. Work with sexual abusers is stressful in itself. Carrying the tensions of this and an abuser's own victimisation throws up added stresses.

Beware! An abuser may be more vulnerable in terms of his risk to himself and others during this stressful phase of assessment.

CHAPTER FOURTEEN

Risk Assessment

The assessment of risk is difficult because of the complexities of individuals and the number of variables which must be considered. However it is also intellectually demanding and professionally satisfying.

Notwithstanding the fact that it is difficult to determine reliable and valid predictors of risk for reasons to be discussed below, there appears an ever increasing demand on those working in this field to produce definitive statements on risk for a variety of purposes. These include opinions in civil proceedings as to the care, supervision and contact of children, in criminal proceedings as to disposal, in mental health review tribunals as to the suitability and necessity for detention, in child protection case conferences considering the desirability and feasibility of family reunification or otherwise, and in the placement of juveniles identified as abusers.

It is as if 'risk assessment' has achieved the status of a discreet entity, the results of which are be treated unquestioningly and without reference to the dynamics of the assessment situation or the person or persons being assessed. Furthermore, some professionals enjoy the professional kudos of 'expert' for it serves their interest to perpetuate the notion of a risk assessment being a definitive process.

We believe that risk assessments have to be based on an understanding of base rates and a clear understanding of relevant research.

At the outset of any attempt to evaluate risk it is imperative that the worker determine the parameters to be examined. We need to ascertain:

(1) Who are the subjects and objects of risk assessment, ie., who, and in what combination are considered as potential abusers, and of whom?

(2) The form of risk to be assessed should be identified including not only issues of direct sexual abuse and indirect sexual abuse (for example genital display, inappropriate boundary setting and the like), but also the broader spectrum of abuses, including emotional abuse, neglect, and physical abuse.

(3) Some idea of the circumstances under which abuse may or may not be expected to occur should be determined, ie., the questions of 'when?' and 'where?'

(4) In addition, and if possible, attempts should be made to describe likely mechanics of abuse, (the 'how?' question) including the potential targeting and grooming procedures which might be used.

Any statement of risk framed on the above should give an indication of the likely validity of the assessment, by highlighting the strengths and weaknesses of the assessment methodologies.

A number of writers (Brearly 1982, Marshall 1990, Moore 1996, Sinclair 1991) draw the important distinction between the probability and cost of the behaviour to be assessed (likelihood of occurrence of the behaviour as opposed to its seriousness). Risk of re-offending and dangerousness are related but are not the same. Moore reminds us of the need to identify possible sources of bias in the assessment process, bias stemming from either the person being assessed, the assessor, or the context within which the assessment is undertaken. Webster and Eaves (1995) offer general principles for improving predictive accuracy in the assessment of dangerousness and risk:

- Referrers should specify what kind of opinion is requested.

- If the worker is aware of bias or lack of expertise the assessment should be declined.

- The predictions should be based on current scientific knowledge.

- It is unlikely that an assessor can make an accurate prediction if it is not possible to estimate the circumstances under which the client would likely be living or the duration of time over which the prediction is expected to hold up.

- Analyses should be based upon a generally known scheme or device.

- Actuarial considerations are important (information should be extracted from historical records which should in turn anchor clinical judgement).

- Information has to be verified.

- The conditions for the assessment have to be adequate (e.g. the assessor should have proper time to do the job, have all the necessary paperwork, and the clients have been properly briefed about the process).

- The information considered should be relevant to the issues.

- Over emphasis on the individual's personality and presentation can be misleading.

- Failure to cross check information from interview sources can introduce error.

- Personal and professional biases should be eliminated to the fullest extent possible.

- Assessment has to be made in the light of 'base rates' for the behaviour (i.e. how often does the behaviour occur in this group of individuals?).
- Predictions should be in specific terms for specific periods.
- Difficult cases may merit a second opinion.

We would argue that before any risk assessment is undertaken a clear model be drawn upon to structure hypotheses about risk and to inform the information gathering and assessment procedures. Risk assessment is an area notoriously fraught with subjective evaluations and a common error is that of making false positive judgements, ie, assuming clients or individuals to be at greater risk, or riskier than is actually the case. Assumptions must be tested and dogma avoided.

A useful model to help assist in the evaluation of risk is that of David Finkelhor's 'Four Factor' Model. The model is useful in as much as it differentiates between motivational factors and maintenance factors. In evaluating risk it is crucial that we find evidence of the person or persons being *motivated* to abuse. With Finkelhor's model in mind therefore initial targets for risk assessment include determination of evidence of sexual arousal to children or child-related stimuli, evidence of the likelihood of emotional needs being met through the abuse of a child, and/or blockage in sustaining age appropriate relationships.

Alongside the determination of motivational factors within the client there are demographic and characterlogical variables which can assist in placing risk within the broader context.

Checklists have been developed to structure information gathering. An example of such is the SVR-2O (Boer *et al.* 1996). These authors indicate a set of 20 factors to consider when assessing the risk of sexual violence, under the headings psychosocial adjustment, sexual offending, and future plans. These are as follows:

Psychosocial Adjustment

(1) Sexual deviation

(2) Victim of child abuse

(3) Psychopathy

(4) Cognitive impairment

(5) Substance use problems

(6) Suicidal/homicidal ideation

(7) Relationship problems

(8) Employment problems

(9) Past nonsexual violent offences

(10) Past nonviolent offences

(11) Past violations of condition release.

Sexual Offending

(12) High density offences

(13) Multiple offence types

(14) Physical harm to victim(s)

(15) Uses weapons or threats of death

(16) Escalation in frequency/severity

(17) Extreme minimisation/denial of offences

(18) Attitudes that support or condone offences.

Future Plans

(19) Lacks realistic plans

(20) Negative attitudes toward intervention.

Despite the increase in the number of programmes in Britain in recent years, the research into recidivism rates still relies heavily on studies carried out in North West America. In trying to predict who will or will not re-offend variables relating to the process of change need to be looked at in two ways. Quinsey and Earls (1990) identified variables which cannot change such as offence history, and those which can, such as sexual preference.

Thornton and Fisher (1993) devised a simple algorithm to work out risk of reoffence levels for the clients in the STEP research (Beckett *et al.* 1994). This was based on the number of sex preconvictions, the number of other preconvictions, any convictions for non-sexual violence and finally the number of victims. They then classified the clients in the following categories; low risk, low-medium risk, medium-high risk, high risk and high+ risk.

One Point for Each of the Following

Any Sex Preconvictions
4+ Preconvictions (Any Kind)
Any Current or Previous Conviction for Non-Sexual Violence
Convicted of Sex Offences Against 3 or More Victims

Risk Categories
No Points   **– Low Risk**
One Point   **– Low–Medium**
Two Points   **– Medium–High**
Three Points – High
Four Points   – High+

Source: Thornton and Travers (1991); Fisher and Thornton (1993)

Figure 14.1 Risk of reconviction algorithm

This algorithm can be useful as a starting point in the risk assessment process where a convicted offender is being assessed. It is of course more limited in civil proceedings where known behaviours have not led to conviction. In addition other factors need to be considered in assessing which lightly convicted offenders may progress to be more heavily convicted.

Quinsey *et al.* (1998) subsequently found that particular measures of anti-sociality were strongly related to recidivism. These factors were psychopathy, criminal history variables and phallometric measures of sexual deviance. Offenders who were psychopathic and sexually deviant were particularly likely to recidivate. In an earlier publication, Quinsey and colleagues (Webster *et al.* 1994) had argued that actuarial measures should be used by clinicians to 'anchor' judgements which might then be modified 'by up to ten per cent when there were compelling circumstances to do so'. In their 1998 text they argue strongly against this, in effect proposing a 'purist' actuarial position. 'What we are advising is not the addition of actuarial methods to existing practice, but rather the complete replacement of existing practice with actuarial methods.' We do not at present propose such a purist approach but do regard actuarial measures as an essential component of risk assessments.

Using Quinsey's original concept of 'anchoring', Thornton (1998) has developed a 'Structured Anchored Clinical Judgement' (SACJ) which has been adopted by many police forces for use in their Sex Offender Act assessments. Stage one of the SACJ is an estimation of high, medium or low risk based on the nature of the previous record, similar to the risk of reconviction algorithm (Figure 14.1). Stage two involves the assessment of combinations of aggravating factors such as male victims, stranger victims, non-contact offences, substance abuse, having been in care, never having lived with an adult partner, deviant arousal and psychopathy. Stage three may involve further aggravating factors such as treatment drop-out, sexual offending related behaviour or deterioration in treatment, or some mitigating factors relevant to progress in treatment and improvement on dynamic (i.e. changeable) factors. The SACJ is a complex assessment tool which requires specific training in its use. It is however a helpful addition to the repertoire of those assessing convicted adult sexual offenders.

Hanson (1997) developed a simpler tool to assess risk of recidivism in convicted adult sexual offenders. This is based on a meta analysis of studies which was replicated on a sample of 2500 sexual offenders. The tool is called the Rapid Risk Assessment of Sex Offender Recidivism (RRASOR). Hanson argues that while it has a slightly lower correlation coefficient than the SACJ the apparent ease of use of the RRASOR may make it more relevant to busy practitioners. Assessors take an offender's risk score on a points system relating to previous sexual offence convictions or charges, age of the offender, whether the offender has ever abused boys, and whether he has had stranger victims. Total scores can range from 0–6. Recidivism rates vary significantly depending on the RRASOR score. Of those scoring 0, 4.4 per cent recidivated after 5 years and 6.5 per cent recidivated after 10 years. However of those scoring 5, 49.8 per cent recidivated after 5 years and 73.1 per cent recidivated after ten years. Again training is necessary for proper administration of the RRASOR.

Hanson and Harris (1997) researched which dynamic variables were found to be relevant in assessing the risk of reoffending. In a sample of 200 offenders who recidivated they found that the following behaviours were statistically significant in the period prior to recidivism:

- disengagement
- manipulativeness
- failing appointments
- drink and drug use
- absences from residence
- feeling low, angry or suffering psychiatric symptoms
- seeing self as a no risk
- sexually disinhibited behaviour
- access to victims
- experiencing a dysfunctional relationship.

Studies prior to Thornton and Hanson had found differing variables. Sinclair (1991) argued that the following were risk factors:

- denial (not confirmed by others but denial does inhibit the success of treatment)
- rapists, exhibitionists, and those who target boys
- contact and non-contact offences
- high impulsivity
- young age for rapists and exhibitionists
- low empathy.

Abel *et al.* (1988) found that a combination of the following five factors accurately predicted recidivism in 85.7 per cent of their sample:

- abuse against both boys and girls
- abuse of victims within and outside the family
- abusers who do not accept increased communication with adults as a goal of treatment
- abusers who are divorced
- abusers who commit both contact and non-contact behaviours.

Many studies also show that the risk of re-offending does not disappear over time. For example Marshall and Barbaree found that after two years the recidivism rate for child sex abusers was 5.5per cent which rose to 25 per cent after four years. For untreated offenders the rates were 12.5 percent after two years rising to 64.3 per cent after four years. The STEP research (Beckett *et al.* 1994) recognized the importance of longer follow up periods and a ten year follow up of the 59 child sex abusers in their study is planned. The two year follow up results were encouraging as noted in Chapter One.

Abusers who drop out of programmes are also considered to be high risk. Abel's (1988) study had the highest drop out rate possibly because he accepted referrals which other programmes refused. It seems that those who drop out of programmes exhibit a high incidence of factors such as impulsivity and lack of recognition of long term risk.

In relation to recidivism rates both Quinsey and Earls (1990) and Marshall (1990) found that race, educational achievement or social class were not significant factors. Quinsey identified pre-treatment deviant sexual interests to be significant in terms of risk but not post treatment deviant interests. The studies of Marshall and his colleagues came to a similar conclusion.

Beckett et al. (1994) attempted to identify varying levels of deviance. The higher deviance group of 26 men had

- committed offences both within the family and outside it

- had tended to commit offences against both boys and girls

- were twice as likely to have committed a previous sexual offence

- had a higher risk of 'reconviction' on the Thornton/Fisher algorithm scale.

- had a much higher rate of being abused as a child.

In drawing the numerous variables together Sinclair (1991) argued that it is helpful to consider the various factors under three headings as follows:

(1) the dangerousness of the crime and the degree of victimization

(2) variables relating to recidivism (described above)

(3) amenability to treatment; the abuser must consider his behaviour to be a problem that he wants to end and he must be willing to take part in a programme specifically designed to address the problems of sexual abuse.

In attempting to develop models to assist practitioners in structuring information, some agencies have found a risk assessment model developed by Brearly (1982) to be helpful. Brearly used the following four headings in his assessment framework:

- **Predisposing Hazards**. These are existing and historical factors which make the danger more likely.

- **Situational Hazards**. These are factors happening currently which make the danger more likely.

- **Strengths**. These are the factors which counteract the danger and make it less likely to become a reality.

- **Dangers**. This section addresses specifically what we want to avoid. It addresses the issue of who is at risk of what and in what circumstances?

Predisposing hazards will include many of the static and actuarial factors mentioned earlier in this chapter. These will relate to criminal record, offence types, deviant arousal, psychopathy, cognitive state, impulsivity, previous supervision record, a record of substance abuse and other factors related to high predictions of recidivism.

Situational factors may relate to changes in the circumstances of the abuser which may influence his behaviour, or provoke changes in him which may alter the risk of his returning to dangerous behaviour. The former might include a move from a hostel where supervision is provided to more lightly supervised accommodation. This might be a particularly critical issue if an abuser is planning to return to a family where he has abused. Potential victims many be more readily accessible and the proximity of children may provoke higher levels of deviant arousal. Situational factors might also include associations with individuals who may not themselves be abusers but might influence the abuser to, say, start drinking, thereby lowering inhibitions. Situational factors with affect mood states and self esteem (e.g. loss of job, financial pressures, relationship difficulties) can also have an influence on arousal patterns and distorted thinking.

Strengths may include internal and external factors. Internal factors may relate to positive responses to supervision where the abuser has acknowledged the nature of his problems and has shown a sustained change in his behaviour, attitudes and feelings over time. In addition he will be able to identify potential high risk situations and be able to plan how to manage them. External factors will include those which enhance stability such as employment, stable accommodation and relationships. They will also include the involvement of others in constraining the abuser's future behaviour. This is more obvious if he is returning to a family, but might also include employers, neighbours and friends.

Dangers need to be assessed specifically in relation to who is in danger of what in what circumstances. Assessors will need to have a view on who the abuser is likely to attack (e.g. women, men, girls, boys or some combination), how he might do it (e.g. by subtle grooming tactics after a long period of targeting an organisation or family or by an apparently sudden attack on a stranger) and in what circumstances (e.g. any time or when specific factors exist such as drinking, mood states, situational influences).

CONCLUDING COMMENTS

Although the task of predicting human behaviour is enormously intricate and subject to considerable error, achieving a thorough understanding of an individual and his circumstances will help to predict the future course of his behaviour (Groth 1978). Sharing information, consulting colleagues and using models and frameworks which have been tested and found useful, will increase our confidence in understanding this difficult task. In addition it is essential that the task is undertaken in a multi-agency, multi-disciplinary context in order to gather all perspectives and protect individual practitioners.

In the area of risk assessment we believe it to be good practice that clients be assessed on more than one occasion, ideally in more than one setting, one of which includes their home. In addition, it is desirable that the client is assessed individually but also interviewed and observed in interaction with significant others. Co-interviewing is desirable, and if possible comments should be recorded verbatim. Sources of information additional to the client and significant others should be drawn upon including where possible social services records and clinical files. It is very easy to under estimate the amount of time involved in thorough risk assessments. It is best to think in terms of days rather than hours for such activity.

The practitioner has a duty to act professionally and as such has a duty not to offer opinions beyond his or her sphere of competence. We would argue that risk assessment is a sophisticated activity requiring quite specialised training. The requirements of time and training are obviously crucial resource issues and managers supporting workers involved in risk assessments need to be aware of this and proactive in supporting professional activity here.

Finally, and whilst it is not the scope of this book to present a text as expert testimony, it is useful at this point to indicate those benchmarks often used to gauge the quality of evidence provided by witnesses to the courts. Myers (1996) poses the following questions:

(1) In formulating an opinion, did the expert consider all relevant facts? How much confidence can be placed in the facts underlying the expert's opinion?

(2) Does the expert have an adequate understanding of pertinent clinical and scientific principles?

(3) To the extent the expert's opinion rests on scientific principles, have the principles been subjected to rigorous testing?

(4) Have the principles or theories relied on by the expert been published in peer-reviewed journals?

(5) Are the principles or theories relied on by the expert generally accepted as reliable by experts in the field?

(6) Did the expert employ appropriate methods of assessment?

(7) Are the inferences and conclusions drawn by the expert defensible?

(8) Is the expert reasonably objective?

Clearly those questions imply standards which are helpful when considering assessment.

References

Abel, G. (1995) *The Abel Assessment of Sexual Interest*. Atlanta: Abel Screening Inc.

Abel, G. and Becker, J. (1985) The Sexual Interest Card Sort. Reproduced in Prentky, R. and Edmunds, S. *Assessing Sexual Abuse. A Resource Guide for Practitioners, 1997*. Brandon: Safer Society Press.

Abel, G., Mittleman, M., Becker, J., Rashner, J. and Aduleau, J. (1988) Predicting Child Molesters' Response to Treatment. *Annals of the New York Academy of Sciences*, 528: 223-34.

All England Law Reports 3rd January 1996 London: Butterworth.

Bandura, A. (1977) *Social Learning Theory*. Englewood Cliffs, NJ: Prentice Hall.

Bartholomew, K. and Horowitz, L.M. (1991) 'Attachment styles among young adults: a test of a four category model.' *Journal of Personality and Social Psychology 61*, 226–244.

Battle, J. (1992) *Culture Free Self-Esteem Inventories*. Austin: Pro-ed.

Bays, L., Freeman-Longo, R. and Hildebran, D. (1990) *How Can I Stop? Breaking My Deviant Cycle*. Orwell: Safer Society Press.

Beckett, R.C. (1994) 'Assessment of sex offenders.' In T. Morrison, M. Erooga and R.C. Beckett *Sexual Offending Against Children*. London: Routledge.

Beckett, R.C., Beech, A., Fisher, D. and Fordham, A.S. (1994) *Community-based Treatment for Sex Offenders: An Evaluation of Seven Treatment Programmes*. London: Home Office.

Bentovim, A. (1988) 'Understanding the phenomenon of sexual abuse – a family systems view of causation.' In A. Bentovim, A. Elton, J. Hildebrand, M. Tranter and E. Vizards (eds) *Child Sexual Abuse Within the Family: Assessment and Treatment. The Work of the Great Ormond Street Sexual Abuse Team*. Bristol: J. Wright.

Boer, D.P., Wilson, R.J., Gauthies, C.M. and Hart, S.D. (1996) 'Assessing risk for sexual violence: guidelines for clinical practice'. Paper presented by D.P. Boer at the 1996 ATSA Conference, Chicago.

Brearley, C.P. (1982) *Risk and Social Work*. London: Routledge and Kegan Paul.

Briggs, D. (1979) 'Penile plethysmographic measurement of sexual arousal in male sexual offenders: effects of instruction of varying stimulus modality upon plethysmographic and related physiological measures.' Unpublished M.Sc thesis, University of Leicester.

Briggs, D. and Lovelock, C. (1993) 'Sexual abuse: the integration of non-abusing partners within perpetrator group therapy'. Paper presented at the 4th European Conference on Child Abuse and Neglect, Padua.

Briggs, F. (ed) (1995) *From Victim to Offender: How Child Sexual Abuse Victims Become Offenders*. St. Leonards: Allen and Unwin.

Bumby, K.M. (1996) 'Assessing the cognitive distortions of child molesters and rapists. Development and valuation of the MOLEST or RAPE scales.' *Sexual Abuse: A Journal of Research and Treatment 8*, 1, 37–54.

Bumby, K. M. (1990) In W.L. Marshall and H.E. Barbaree (eds) *Handbook of Sexual Assault. Issues, Theories, and Treatment of the Offender*. New York: Plenum.

Burt, M.R. (1980) 'Cultural myths and supports for rape.' *Journal of Psychology and Sexual Psychology 38*, 217–230.

Butler-Sloss Rt. Hon. Lord Justice (1988) Report of the Inquiry into Child Abuse in Cleveland, 1987, London: HMSO, Cmnd 412.

Butts Stahly, G. (1997) 'The abuse continues. Custody conflicts in the family violence scenario'. Paper presented at the San Diego Conference on Responding to Child Maltreatment, San Diego.

Campbell, J.C. (ed) (1995) *Assessing Dangerousness: Violence by Sexual Offenders, Batterers and Child Abusers.* London: Sage.

Card, R. (1996) *The Sexual Projecture Card Set (SPCS): A Projectural Apperception Test for Sexual Issues, Sexual Offenders or Victims.* Behavioural Technology Inc.

Carich, M. and Adkerson, L. (1997) 'Victim empathy and resource inventory.' In R. Prentky and S.B. Edmunds. *Assessing Sexual Abuse. A Resource Guide for Practitioners.* Brandon: Safer Society Press.

Cavanagh Johnson, T. (1997) *Child Sexuality Curriculum for Abused Children and Their Parents.* From Toni Cavanagh Johnson, 1101 Fremont Avenue, South Pasadena, California.

Chaffin, M. (1997) 'Managing teen offenders: unsupportive families and family reunification. San Diego, California. APSAC 1997 Advanced Training Institutes, January.

Chambless, D.L. and Lifshitz, L. (1984) 'Self reported sexual anxiety and arousal: the expanded sexual arousability inventory.' *The Journal of Sex Research 20*, 241–254.

Check, J.V.P. (1985) 'The hostility towards women scale' (Doctoral Dissertation, University of Monitoba, 1984) Dissertation Abstracts International, 45, (12).

Conte, Wolf, S. and Smith, T. (1989) 'What sex offenders tell us about perpetration strategies.' *Child Abuse and Neglect 13*, 293–301.

Corbett, A. (1996) *Trinity of Pain. Therapeutic Responses to People with Learning Disabilities who Commit Sexual Offences.* London: Respond.

Cowburn, M., Wilson, C. and Loewenstein, P. (1992) *Changing Men: A Practice Guide to Working with Adult Male Sexual Offenders.* Nottingham: Nottinghamshire Probation Service.

Cronbach, L. (1969) *Essentials of Psychological Testing*, (3rd Edition). London: Harper and Row.

Cumming, G. and Buell, M. (1997) *Supervision of the Sex Offender.* Brandon: Safer Society Press.

Davis, M. H.(1997) 'Interpersonal reactivity index.' In R. Prentky and S.B. Edmunds. *Assessing Sexual Abuse. A Resource Guide for Practitioners.* Brandon: Safer Society Press.

Davis, M.H. (1980) 'A multi-dimensional approach to individual differences in empathy.' *J.S.A.S. Catalogue of Selected Documents in Psychology 10*, 85.

Deitz, S.R. (1992) 'Measurement of empathy towards rape, victims and rapists.' *Journal of Personality and Social Psychology 43*, 372–384.

Doyle, P. and Gooch, T. (1995) 'The mentally handicapped as offenders.' *Forensic Aspects of Mental Health.* Basingstoke: Merit Publishers.

Dunkerley, A., Doyle, P., Gooch, T. and Kennington, R. (1994) 'Learning from perpetrators of child sexual abuse.' *Probation Journal 41*, 3, 147–151.

Earle, R.H., Earle, M.R. and Osborn, K. (1995) *Sex Addiction Case Studies and Management*. New York: Brunner and Mazel.

Ehrenberg, M.F. and Elterman, M.F. (1995) 'Evaluating Allegations of Sexual Abuse in the Context of Divorce, Child Custody and Access Disputes'. In Tara Ney (Ed.) *True and False Allegations of Child Sexual Abuse: Assessment and Case Management*. New York: Brunner/Mazel.

Ellis, L. (1989) *Theories of Rape: Inquiries into the Causes of Sexual Aggression*. New York: Hemisphere Publishing Corporation.

Faller, K.C. (1993) *Child Sexual Abuse: Interaction and Treatment Issues*. Washington: US Department of Health and Human Services (National Centre on Child Abuse and Neglect).

Field, H.S. (1978) 'Attitudes toward rape: a comparative analysis of police, rapists, crisis-councellors, and citizens.' *Journal of Personality and Social Psychology 36*, 156–179.

Finkelhor, D. and Associates (1986) *A Sourcebook on Child Sexual Abuse*. California: Sage.

Fisher, D. (1995) Paper delivered to NOTA Conference, Cambridge.

Fisher, D. (1994) 'Adult sex offenders: who are they? How and why do they do it?' In T. Morrison, M. Erooga and R.C. Beckett. *Sexual Offending Against Children*. London: Routledge.

Freud, S. (1925) 'Three essays on the theories of sexuality.' In *The Complete Works of Sigmund Freud*. London: Hogarth Press.

Freund, K. (1990) 'Courtship disorder'. In Marshall, W.L., Barbaree, H. and Laws, D.R. (1990) *Handbook of Sexual Assault*. New York: Plennum Press.

Freund, K. and Kolarsky, A. (1965) 'Grundzuge eines einfachen bezugsystems fur die analyse sexueller deviationen' (Basic features of a reference system for considering anomalous erotic preferences). *Psychiatrie, neurologie and medizinische Psychologie, 17*, 221–225.

Furby, L., Weinrott, M.R. and Blackshaw, L. (1989) 'Sex offender recidivism: a review.' *Psychological Bulletin 105*, 3–30.

Gardiner, D. and Talbot, J. (1990) *Dependency Manual*. Newcastle: Northumbria Probation Service.

George, W. and Marlatt, G. (1989) 'Introduction to relapse prevention with sexual offenders.' In D.R. Laws (ed) *Relapse Prevention with Sexual Offenders*. New York: Guilford Press.

Gilyeat, D. (1993) *A Companion Guide to Offence Seriousness*. Iikley: Owen Wells.

Gordon, A. (1996) 'Improving the impact of treatment: applying principles of effective correctional treatment to sex offenders'. Paper presented at the 1996 ATSA Conference, Chicago.

Groth, A.N. (1979) *Men Who Rape. The Psychology of the Offender*. New York: Plenum.

Groth, A.N. and Burgess, A.W. (1980) 'Male rape: offenders and victims.' *American Journal of Psychiatry 137*, 806–10.

Grubin, D. and Gunn, J. (1990) *The Imprisoned Rapist and Rape*. London: Institute of Psychiatry.

Hall, E.R., Howard, J.A. and Boezio, S.L. (1986) 'Tolerance of rape: a sexist or antisocial attitude.' *Psychology of Women Quarterly 10*, 101–118.

Hall, G. (1995) 'Sexual offender recidivism revisited: a meta-analysis of recent treatment studies.' *Journal of Consulting and Clinical Psychology 63*, 5, 802–809.

Hall, G.C.N. (1990) Prediction of Sexual Aggression. *Clinical Psychology Review 10*, 229–245.

Hall, G.C.N., Hirchman, R., Graham, J.R. and Zaragoza, M.J. (eds) (1993) *Sexual Aggression: Issues in Etiology, Assessment and Treatment.* Washington, DC: Taylor and Francis.

Hanson, R.K. (1997) *Development of a Brief Actuarial Risk Scale for Sexual Offense Recidivism.* Ottawa: Department of Solicitor General of Canada.

Hanson, R.K., Gizzarelli, R. and Scott, H. (1994) 'The attitudes of incest offenders: sexual entitlement and acceptance of sex with children.' *Criminal Justice and Behaviour 21*, 2, 187–20.

Hanson, R.K. and Harris, A.J.R. (1997) *Dynamic Predictors of Sexual Reoffense Project.* Ottawa: Department of Solicitor General of Canada.

Haven, J. Little, R. and Petre-Mille, D. (1990) *Treating Intellectually Disabled Sex Offenders: A Model Residential Program.* Orwell: Safer Society Press.

Hedderman, C. and Sugg, D. (1996) 'Does creating sex offenders reduce reoffending?' *Home Office Research and Statistics Department Research Findings No.45.*

Herman, J.L. (1990) 'Sex offenders: a feminist perspective.' In W.L. Marshall, D.R. Laws and H.E. Barbaree. *Handbook of Sexual Assault.* New York: Plenum Press.

Hogan, R. (1969) 'Development of an empathy scale'. *Journal of Consulting and Clinical Psychology 33*, 307–316.

Hollins, C.R. and Howells, K. (1991) *Clinical Approaches to Sex Offenders and their Victims.* Chichester: John Wiley and Sons.

Home Office (1992) *National Standards for the Supervision of Offenders in the Community.* London: Home Office.

Home Office (1995) *National Standards for the Supervision of Offenders in the Community.* London: Home Office.

Home Office (1997) *Home Office Circular 39/1997.* London: Home Office.

Home Office (1997) *Sex Offenders Act.* London: Her Majesty's Stationery Office.

Home Office, Department of Health, Department of Education and Science, Welsh Office (1991) *Working Together.* London: Her Majesty's Stationery Office.

Hildebran, D. and Pithers, W.O. (1989) 'Enhancing offender empathy for sexual-abuse victims.' In D.R. Laws (ed) *Relapse Prevention with Sex Offenders.* New York: The Guilford Press.

H.M. Prison Service (1994) 'Release of prisoners convicted of offences against children or young persons under the age of 18' Guidance Notes to: Instruction to Governors. 54/1994.

Jenkins, A. (1990) *Invitations to Responsibility.* Adelaide: Dulwich Centre Publications.

Jones, R. (1996) *Mental Health Act Manual.* London: Sweet and Maxwell.

Knight, R.A. and Prentky, R.A. (1990) 'Classifying sexual offenders: the development and corroboration of taxonomic models.' In W.L. Marshall, D.R. Laws and H.E. Barbaree *Handbook of Sexual Assault.* New York: Plenum Press.

Knight, R.A., Prentky, R.A. and Cerce, D. (1994) 'The development, reliability and validity of an inventory for the multidimensional assessment of sex or aggression.' *Criminal Justice and Behaviour 21*, 72–94.

Koss, M.P. and Leonard, K.E. (1984) 'Sexually aggressive men: empirical findings and theoretical implications.' In N. Malamuth and E. Donnerstein. *Pornography and Sexual Aggression.* New York: Academic Press.

Koss, M.P. or Oros, C. (1982) 'Sexual experiences survey. A research instrument investigating sexual aggression and victimisation.' *Journal of Consulting and Clinical Psychology 50*, 455–457.

Lanyon, R.I. (1991) 'Theories of sex offending.' In C.R. Hollin and K. Howells. *Clinical Approaches to Sex Offenders and their Victims.* Chichester: John Wiley and Sons.

Leonard, P. (1975 'Towards a paradigm for radical practice.' *In R. Bailey and M. Brake. Radical Social Work.* London: Arnold.

Levison, B. (1997) 'Victim empathy scale.' In R. Prentky and S.B. Edmunds. *Assessing Sexual Value. A Resource Guide for Practitioners.* Brandon: Safer Society Press.

Lottes, I.L. (1988) 'Rape supportive attitude scale.' In C.M. Davis, W.L. Yarbes and S.L. Davis (eds) *Sexuality Related Measures: A Compendium.* Iowa: Graphic Publishing Company.

McColl, A. and Hargreaves, R. (1992) 'Explaining sex offending in court reports.' *Probation Journal 40*, 1.

McGuire, J. (1995) *What Works: Reducing Reoffending, Guidelines from Research and Practice.* Chichester: John Wiley and Sons.

McGuire, J. and Priestly, P. (1985) *Offending Behaviour, Skills and Strategies for Going Straight.* London: Betsford Academic.

McMullen, R.J. (1990) *Male Rape: Breaking the Silence on the Last Taboo.* London: Gay Men's Press.

Malamuth, N.M. (1981) 'Rape proclivity among males.' *Journal of Social Issues 37*, 138–57.

Malamuth, N.M. (1989) 'The Attraction to Sexual Aggression Scale: Part 1'. *Journal of Sex Research 26*, 26–49.

Malamuth, N.M. (1989) 'The Attraction to Sexual Aggression Scale: Part 2'. *Journal of Sex Research 26*, 324–354.

Malamuth, M.N., Heavey, C.L. and Linz, D. (1993) 'Predicting men's anti social behaviour against women; the interaction model of sexual aggression.' In G.C.N. Hall, R. Hirchman, J.R. Graham and M.S. Zarogoza (eds) *Sexual Aggression, Issues in Etiology, Assessment and Treatment.* Washington DC: Taylor and Francis Publisher.

Malamuth, M.N., Barnes, G., Heavey, C.L. and Linz, D. (1995) 'Using the confluence model of sexual aggression to predict men's conflict with women: a ten-year follow-up study'. *Journal of Personality and Social Psychology 69*, 2, 353–439.

Maletzky, B.M. (1990) *Treating the Sexual Offender.* California: Sage.

Marlatt, G.A. (1985) 'Cognitive assessment and intervention procedures for relapse prevention.' In G.A. Marlatt and J.R. Gordon (eds) *Relapse Prevention – Maintenance Strategies in the Treatment of Addictive Behaviours.* New York: Guildford.

Marshall, K. and Weaver, P. (1991) *Targets for Change.* Nottingham: Nottinghamshire Probation Service.

Marshall, W.L. (1995) Intimacy, Attachment and Loneliness: Their Theoretical Relevance, Measurement and Treatment. Seminar NOTA/ATSA Conference, Cambridge.

Marshall, W.L. (1993) 'A revised approach to the treatment of men who sexually assault adult females.' In G.C.N. Hall, R. Hirchman, J.R. Graham and M.S. Zarogoza (eds) *Sexual Aggression, Issues in Etiology, Assessment and Treatment.* Washington, DC: Francis and Taylor.

Marshall, W.L. (1989) 'Intimacy, loneliness and sexual offending.' *Behaviour Research and Therapy 27,* 5, 491–503.

Marshall, W.L. and Barbaree, H.E. (1990) 'An integrated theory of the etiology of sexual offending.' In W.L. Marshall, D.R. Laws and H.E. Barbaree (eds) *Handbook of Sexual Assault.* New York: Plenum Press.

Marshall, W.L. and Barbaree, H.E. (1990) 'Outcome of comprehensive cognitive behavioural programmes'. In W.L. Marshall, D.R. Laws and H.E. Barbaree (eds) *Handbook of Sexual Assault.* New York: Plenum Press.

Mayfield, D. and McLeon Gard Hall P. *American Journal of Psychology 131,* 21–3.

Mehrabian, A. and Epstein, N. (1972) A measure of emotional empathy. *Journal of Personality 40,* 525–543.

Mental Health Act (1983) London: HMSO.

Miller, W., Rollnick, S. (1995) *Motivational Interviewing: Preparing People to Change Addictive Behaviour.* New York: Guilford Press.

Moore, B. (1996) *Risk Assessment: A Practitioner's Guide to Predicting Harmful Behaviour.* London: Whiting and Brich Ltd.

Morrison, T. (1993) *Staff Supervision in Social Care.* UK: Longman.

Morrison, T. (1990) 'The emotional effects of child protection work on the worker.' *Practice Volume 4,* No.4, 253–271. Birmingham: B.A.S.W.

Morrison, T. and Print, B. (1995) *Adolescent Sexual Abusers: An Overview.* Hull: NOTA (the National Association for the Development of Work with Sex Offenders).

Mosher, D.L. and Sirkin, M. (1984) 'Measuring in a macho personality constellation.' *Journal of Research in Personality 18,* 150–164.

Murphy, W.D. (1990) 'Assessment and modification of cognitive distortions.' In W.L. Marshall, D.R. Laws and H.E. Barbaree (eds) *Handbook of Sexual Assault.* New York: Plenum Press.

Myers, J.E.B. (1996) 'Expert testimony.' In J. Briere, L. Berliner, J.A. Bulkely, C. Jenny and T. Redi (eds) *The APSAC Handbook on Child Maltreatment.* London: Sage.

Nelson, C. and Jackson, P. (1989) 'High risk recognition: the cognitive behavioural chain.' In D.R. Laws. *Relapse Prevention with Sex Offenders.* Guildford Press.

Nichols, H.R. and Molinder, I. (1984) Multiphasic Sex Inventory Manual (Available from Nichols and Molinder, 437 Bowes Drive, Tacoma WA 98466, USA)

Noelly, D., Muccigrosso, L. and Zigman, E. (1996) 'Treatment successes with mentally retarded sex offenders'. In E. Coleman, S.M. Dwyer and N.J. Pallone. *Sex Offender Treatment: Biological Dysfunction, Intrapsychic Conflict, Interpersonal Violence.* New York: Haworth Press.

Oliver, L.L. and Chambers, K. (1993) 'Introduction: etiology and assessment.' In G.C.N. Hall, R. Hirchman, J.R. Graham and M.J. Zaragoza (eds) *Sexual Aggression: Issues in Etiology Assessment and Treatment*. Washington DC: Taylor and Francis.

Paitich, D. (1977) 'The Clark SHQ: a clinical sex history questionnaire for males.' *Archives of Sexual Behaviour 6*, 421–426.

Perkins, D. (1991) 'Clinical work with sex offenders in secure settings.' In C. Hollin and K. Howells. *Clinical Approaches to Sex Offenders and their Victims*. New York: Wiley.

Pithers, W.D. (1993) 'Treatment of rapists: reinterpretation of early outcome data and exploratory constructs to enhance therapeutic efficacy.' In G.C.N. Hall, R. Hirshman, J.R. Graham and M.S. Zarogoza. *Sexual Aggression, Issues in Etiology, Assessment and Treatment*. Washington DC: Taylor and Francis.

Pithers, W.D. (1990) 'Relapse prevention and sexual aggressors: a method for maintaining therapeutic gain and enhancing external supervision.' In W.L. Marshall, D.R. Laws and H.E. Barbaree. *Handbook of Sexual Assault*. New York: Plenum Press.

Pokomy, A., Miller, B.A. and Kaplan, H.B. (1972) *American Journal of Psychiatry 129*, 342–5.

Prentky, R. and Edmunds, S.B. (1997) *Assessing Sexual Abuse: A Resource Guide for Practitioners*. Brandon: Safer Society Press.

Prochaska, J. and Di Clemente, C. (1982) 'Transtheoretical therapy: toward a more integrative model of change.' *Psychotherapy: Theory, Research and Practice 19*, 3.

Proctor, E. (1994) *The Sex Offence Attitudes Questionnaire*. Oxford: Oxford Probation Service.

Quinsey, V.L. and Earls, C.M. (1990) 'The modification of sexual preferences.' In W.L. Marshall, D.R. Laws and H.E. Barbaree (eds) *Handbook of Sexual Assault Issues, Theories and Treatment of the Offender*. New York: Plennum Press.

Quinsey, V.L., Harris, G.T., Rice, M.E. and Cormier, C.A. (1998) *Violent Offenders: Appraising and Managing Risk*. Washington: American Psychological Association.

Rasmussen, L.A., Burton, J.E. and Christopherson, B.J. (1992) 'Precursors to offending and the trauma outcome in sexually reactive children.' *Journal of Child Sexual Abuse 1*.

R v Cunnah (1996) *Criminal Law Review* January 1996. London: Sweet and Maxwell.

Russell, D., Peplau, L.A. and Cutrona, C.A. (1980) 'The revised U.C.L.A. loneliness scale: concurrent and discriminant validity evidence.' *Journal of Personality and Social Psychology 39*, 472–480.

Ryan, G. (1989) 'Victim to victimiser: rethinking victim treatment.' *Journal of Interpersonal Violence 4*, 3, 325–341.

Ryan, G., Lane, S.R., Davis, J.M. and Isaac, C.B. (1987) 'Juvenile sex offenders: development and correction.' *Child Abuse and Neglect 2*, 385–95.

Ryan, L. and Lane, S.C. (1991) 'The impact of sexual abuse on the interventionist.' In L. Ryan and S. Lane. *Juvenile Sexual Offending: Causes, Consequences and Corrections*. Lexington Books.

Salter, A. (1988) *Treating Child Sex Offenders and Victims – A Practical Guide*. California: Sage.

Scottish Office (1997) *Circular SWSG 11/97*. Edinburgh Scottish Office.

Scully, D. (1990) *Understanding Sexual Violence*. Boston: Unwin Hyman.

Segal, Z.V. and Stermac, L.E. (1990) 'The role of cognition in sexual assault.' In W.L. Marshall, D.R. Laws and H.E. Barbaree. *Handbook of Sexual Assault*. New York: Plenum Press.

Sentence Management and Planning: An Operational Guide for the Prison and Probation Services (1997): Prison Service Orders 2200.

Sheikh, A.A. (ed) (1983) *Imagery: Current Theory, Research and Application*. New York: Wiley.

Sinclair, L. (1991) 'Assessment: a comprehensive task. Assessing risk; effective interviewing'. Presentation to ROTA Conference, Liverpool.

Singer, J.L. and Antrobus, J.S. (1972) 'Daydreaming, imaginal processes, and personality: a normative study.' In P.W. Sheehan (ed) *The Function and Nature of Imagery*. New York: Academic Press.

Smith, G. (1994) 'Parent, partner, protector: conflicting role demands for mothers of sexually abused children.' In T. Morrison, M. Erooga and R.C. Beckett (eds) *Sexual Offending Against Children*. London: Routledge.

Spence, J. and Helmreich, R. (1972) 'The attitudes towards women scale: an objective instrument to measure attitudes toward the rights and roles of women in contemporary society.' *Psychological Documents 2*, 153.

Stanfield, J. (1990) *Life Facts 1: Sexuality*. Santa Barbara, CA: James Stanfield.

Stone, N. (1996) *A Companion Guide to Life Sentences*. Iikley: Wells.

Stone, N. (1996) 'P.S.R.'s: new version of offence.' *Probation Journal 43*, 1.

Stone, N. (1993) *Criminal Offences, Definitions, Penalties and Sentencing Guidance*. Norwich: University of East Anglia.

Strauss, M.A. (1979) 'Measuring intrafamily conflict and violence: the conflict tactics (CT) scales.' *Journal of Marriage and the Family 41*, 75–88.

Summit, R. (1983) 'The child sexual abuse accommodation syndrome.' *Child Abuse and Neglect 7*, 177–193.

Thornton, D. (1994) 'Self-esteem questionnaire'. In R.C. Beckett, A. Beech, D. Fisher and A.S. Fordham. *Community-based Treatment for Sex Offenders: An Evaluation of Seven Treatment Programmes*. London: Home Office.

Thornton, D. (1998) Personal communications.

Thornton, D. and Fisher, D. (1994) In R.C. Beckett, A. Beech, D. Fisher and A.S. Fordham. *Community Based Treatment for Sex Offenders: An Evaluation of Seven Treatment Programmes*. London: Home Office.

Tieger, T. (1981) 'Self-rated likelihood of raping and social perception of rape.' *Journal of Research in Personality 15*, 147–58.

Webster, C.D. and Eaves, D. (1995) *The HCR-20 Scheme: The Assessment of Dangerousness and Risk: Version 1, January 1995* Monograph from Simon Fraser. University and Forensic Psychiatric Services Commission of British Columbia.

Webster, C.D., Harris, G.T., Rice, M.E., Cormier, C.A. and Quinsey, V.L. (1994) *The Violence Prediction Scheme Assessing Dangerousness in High-Risk Men*. Toronto: University of Toronto, Centre of Criminology.

White, R. (1996) 'The standards of proof in care proceedings.' *Child Abuse Review 5*, 67–69.

Willis, G.C. (1993) *Unspeakable Crimes*. London: The Children Society.

Wilson, G. (1978) *The Secrets of Sexual Fantasy*. London: Dent.

Wolf, S.C. (1991) *Advanced Practice Skills Workshop*. Chester.

Wolf, S.C. (1988) 'A model of sexual aggression/addiction.' *Journal of Social Work and Human Sexuality 7*, 1.

Wolf, S.C. (1985) 'A multi factor model of deviant sexuality.' *Victimology: An International Journal 10*, 359–74.

Woolf, The Right Honourable Lord Justice (1990) 'Report of an enquiry into prisoner disturbance April 1990'. HMSO CM 1946.

Subject Index

Author Index